THE FAITHFUL MANAGER

USING YOUR **GOD GIVEN** TOOLS FOR
WORKPLACE SUCCESS

ANTHONY E. SHAW

Aventine Press

Published by Aventine Press
55 East Emerson St.
Chula Vista CA 91911
www.aventinepress.com

ISBN: 978-1-59330-820-9

Library of Congress Control Number: 2013907580
Library of Congress Cataloging-in-Publication Data
The Faithful Manager / Anthony E. Shaw

Printed in the United States of America
ALL RIGHTS RESERVED

TABLE OF CONTENTS

"A man's true estate of power and riches is to be in himself; not in his dwelling or position or external relations, but in his own essential character."

Henry Ward Beecher (1813 – 1887)

"Sometimes intellect doesn't equate to wisdom."

Andrew Imparato (Advocate for the disabled, quoted at the Genetics and Public Policy Center)

For

Emma Rose, Gabriel Victor, Ethan Anthony

and

all my nieces and nephews

who teach me about God's Love everyday

Thank you

Prologue

Why this book?

One of the inspirations for writing this book was a remark I heard attributed to the late musician George Harrison. After the Beatles went their separate paths, Harrison performed and produced his own music and continued a personal journey of spiritual discovery that lasted until his death in December 2001. Commenting on his faith, he stated **"Everything else can wait, but the search for God cannot wait . . ."**

We live and work in times of great challenge; times that seem drastically unlike much of the recent past. The 1960s, 70s, 80s and even the 90s are tranquil, distant memories in comparison to now. Our childhoods appear to us now as more innocent than our children's. Marriages seem to have been more stable and our work lives more predictable. The events of the world, it seems, were more ordered and less random in nature.

We live amid a current culture in which the mainstream media routinely ridicules citizens who express their belief that praying for America's recovery is a powerful tool. Where 10,000,000 viewers watch an aerialist walk across Niagara Falls, while the broadcast network willfully ignores and refuses to report the fact that he is praying during the entire event. We see violence masquerading as protest. Where pornography and obscenity are celebrated as protected speech. A world where license is mistaken for liberty and fame is confused with genius. Value appears to have replaced values. We no longer disagree with other people; we hate them for disagreeing with us. Being bitter has replaced having self-responsibility. Popular is the yardstick for measuring what is correct. Sex really isn't sex and a lie really isn't a lie. Rudeness equals dialogue. Abnormal is the new, venerated normal. The definitions of long held beliefs, we are informed by some, now need to be turned upside down.

What we experience in the present world often rattles our foundations, literally and figuratively, at home, abroad and at work. In the midst of this tumult, we go to work and we try our best to manage through the day. We depend on our leaders, colleagues and teammates at work to help us meet our own goals and those of our organizations.

Our faith is on the line every day.

At times, we experience a direct frontal assault as our faith is questioned and challenged openly. At other times, these challenges are more subtle. We become involved, perhaps unwillingly and unknowingly, in situations that require us to put our reliance and trust in our faith on the line.

> **"No less a figure than the Rev. Billy Graham has predicted that 'one of the next great moves of God is going to be through believers in the workplace.' "**

As a human resources professional, I see managers struggling to interpret the changing world of work, cope with government regulations and laws, understand the motives and actions of co-workers, and try to produce positive results consistently. It isn't simple anymore (if it ever was)! Everyday I support, coach, counsel, guide, mentor and sometimes help discipline managers – it's my living but it's also my passion. Helping others to succeed is one of life's biggest blessings.

I believe that in and outside of the workplace, it is our faith that is being tested.

Much of what managers feel stands in the way of their succeeding at managing people (and managing themselves) is a challenge to their faith. Faith as a concept and as a practice is under attack. Every conflicting issue I cited above illustrates a particular battle in this assault on faith.

> **"People are realizing their faith can help interpret where we spend most of our waking hours."**

Of all the books for managers that I've read, none have combined the elements of faith, values, shared humanity and best practices advice. Ahead on the list of business best practices is faith. The purpose of this book is to strengthen the armor of your faith and sharpen your practical use of that faith in your workplace. To be a manager, to manage yourself and your co-workers successfully is to be an officer in the army of the faithful – the good soldiers who get up every morning, go to work, give an honest and productive day, and return to the task tomorrow.

"Spirituality in the workplace is exploding."

In the final analysis, Mr. Harrison was correct; the search for our faith and our connection with the Creator of that faith cannot be denied or postponed in the workplace or anyplace else.

Lesson:

"It doesn't matter what you call Him just as long as you call." George Harrison

Chapter One
The First Word

We do well always and everywhere to have faith.

Faith in ourselves and in our shared humanity with our colleagues. Faith in others, in their essential dignity and self-worth, and in our need for them and their efforts in order for all of us to survive, prosper and be successful. ***Faith in our Creation.***

Throughout this book I will talk with you about leadership, respect, authenticity and many other aspects of being a successful manager. What you will hear is my faith in you as a successful person. I can't see you and you will likely only ever see a photograph of me. Most probably, I will never have the opportunity to know you individually. Where I go in life and where you go will probably not be known to each other. In spite of that, I still have that faith in you. Faith is what you believe in with all your mind and spirit without having to be shown the proof because the proof is manifest.

> **"It is the evidence of things we cannot yet see."**
> *Hebrews 11:1*

In what do you have faith?
You and I have a journey. In this book, we share a journey that goes deep within ourselves and explores what motivates us, what we feel, hear, see and think as we manage the workday.

We have another important journey. This is our personal journey through life. While this journey is uniquely our own, we share it with everyone else - each of us taking that unique personal journey, though we are never truly alone. ***This is our greatest task, to live a life that is rich and textured, long and rewarding, and, in the end meaningful.***

5

So much of that journey is traveled at work, that how we each live our work life accounts for a significant portion of our life's meaning and reward. The director and choreographer (and granddaughter of Duke Ellington) Mercedes Ellington stated,

"We take many journeys in life. Some are pleasant and some are painful and some take us back to where we began."

I started life in the borough of Queens in New York City in 1955. My mom was unwed when I was born and she already had a six-year old son, my older brother Lee. She was a twenty-six year old nurse's aide when I entered the picture and she was responsible for raising two sons, by herself. I know that she lived on her own, although my maternal grandmother, a large and imposing woman of Native- and African-American descent, also lived in New York City, in Brooklyn. When I was five, my mother met and married the love of her life, my stepfather Carleton Shaw, who was 29 years her senior.

To this day I've never met my biological father and I have only meager clues to his name. But my stepfather, along with my mother, raised me from age five until his death when I was twenty-one. I gained two beloved younger brothers in the interim, Carl, Jr. and John.

We were four boys with our mom and dad in the Bedford-Stuyvesant section of Brooklyn during the hectic 1960s and 70s. As a family we weren't poor but we were often broke! There wasn't a lot of money in our household. There was, however, more than enough love, nurturing, respect, dignity and encouragement for learning.

Both of our parents revered learning. Our home was filled with books. Our parents expected us to know about politics and art. We knew to always say "thank you" and "please." We took family outings to museums and libraries and public gardens. During the election night of 1972, my stepfather returned home from work late in the evening and announced, "I'm going out to vote for the loser," because he believed in the candidate's message and to demonstrate that even in the face of sure defeat, it was important to do what he felt was the right thing to do.

I attended New York City public schools, as did all of my brothers, and was graduated from the business school of the City University system, Bernard M. Baruch College. I commuted to classes in Manhattan by subway. My first years of college were free because at that time, City University didn't charge tuition for New York City high school graduates. This is now ancient history!

My stepfather died while I was attending college (the same college he attended for adult ed courses), so for my junior and senior years I took over his last job doing maintenance and repair work for a landlord in the Brooklyn Heights neighborhood. Eventually I was hired by Dun & Bradstreet and then by the landlord agency of the U.S. government, the General Services Administration, as an Urban Planner. I subsequently worked for the New York City Department of Investigation; the nation's largest animal welfare charity; the Mayor of the City of Yonkers, New York; the largest air freight company in North America; and several other private and not-for-profit organizations. I have helped investigate the biggest scandal in New York City history, worked to clean up one of the most corrupt municipal governments in the U.S., managed the acquisition and merger of the only animal poison control center in the U.S., and counseled managers on everything from harassment in the workplace to failed marriages.

Along the way I've traveled the world, from walking on the Great Wall of China to jogging in the Alps. My salary in one year was more than my parents had been paid in salaries in their entire lives. As a young man I avoided eye contact with police officers because I feared being noticed by them as a Black male in an urban ghetto. Years later I would be sworn in as the City of Yonkers' first Deputy Mayor of African-American descent, with management responsibility for the Police Commissioner, among others.

At a certain point later in my life, I suddenly stopped and realized what a miracle of faith my life had been. I recall my mother, a chronic asthmatic whose trying life was ended by cancer at age 49, repeating one phrase whenever she dipped into her reserve of faith for strength; **"God is good."**

Jump forward to the present.

Riding home one afternoon in my car, my first son and I began talking about miracles. I don't remember how we came to that topic but I recall it was preceded by us talking about his feelings about inviting a friend to his birthday party. Gabriel asked me, "Have any miracles happened?" Of course, when I quickly replied "Yes," he wanted details! I had to think for a moment before I could answer truthfully.

I told him he was a miracle. Our doctor informed my then wife and me that after the birth of our first child Emma, the odds weren't on our side for another pregnancy. The birth of our daughter had followed a long and anxious road. The gift of Gabriel came unexpectedly almost two years after Emma's birth.

Indeed, he is living, breathing miracle.

"What other miracles have happened?"

I told him about Nachum Sasonkin. I'm looking at a photograph of Nachum as I write. He is a handsome, bright-eyed young man of the Lubavitcher sect in Brooklyn. In March 2004, he was graduated from the Rabbinical College of America and ordained a rabbi. He carried with him to his ordination a bullet lodged in his brain. Ten years before his ordination, Nachum was an 18 year old student, riding in a van with his school friends, approaching the Brooklyn Bridge. A deranged hate-filled man, blinded by anti-Semitism, fired a gun into the van, killing another passenger, Ari Halberstam, and severely wounding Nachum.

"For months, (Nachum) lived on a respirator, communicating by blinking once for 'yes' and twice for 'no,' and being fed by a tube through his stomach."

While his doctors doubted he would ever walk or talk again, Nachum's family and friends, and the faith-filled community to which he belonged, stayed by his side. They took shifts sitting at his bedside, talking to him, singing to him, praying with the faith that a miracle would occur.

Listen to how Rabbi Sasonkin describes his personal miracle:

"I thank God for allowing me to recognize the preciousness of each breath and step I take. I pray that I continue to lead my life on a deeper level than I did before, never taking anything for granted, always recognizing His blessings."

I told Gabriel about Gabrielle Acevedo. I'm also looking at a photograph of her. Gabrielle had leukemia. She was in the second grade in the Bronx. In the photograph little Gabrielle is asleep in a hospital bed with numerous tubes attached to her. She was born with heart disease and was diagnosed in 2003 with an acute leukemia strain.

Before you feel sorry for her, listen to what her teacher Rochelle Moche, another extraordinary person, says she learned when Gabrielle insisted upon receiving her school assignments on the day of her bone marrow transplant:

"(Gabrielle) wipes off her nose, finishes throwing up and does the assignment. I learned humility, I learned how to listen, and I'll remember that for the rest of my life."

Gabrielle has written words to a published picture book entitled "A Boy, A Dog and A Frog." The book is full of hope and happiness. Although Gabrielle eventually lost her battle with leukemia, she won the battle to live in faith. Gabrielle, Nachum, Gabriel and Emma are miraculous human beings, full of faith and testaments to faith's power.

The Necessity of Faith

Faith is more powerful in the world and in the workplace than any other force - ambition, passion, despair or greed. A Christian commentator remarked that he sees many Christians who are afraid to talk about their faith, as if stating you have faith is somehow embarrassing. The same attitude can be found in some Jews, Muslims and the faithful in other religions.

Have faith in miracles and you will be in enviable company.

"A national survey of 1,100 physicians . . . found that 74% of doctors believe that miracles have occurred in the past and 73% believe they can occur today."

I had a discussion with a neighbor about faith in the workplace. I guess you could characterize the discussion as a disagreement. I said successful managers need to have faith. He said he was suspicious of anyone who made a big deal about having faith because more wars had been started and people killed over conflicts about faith than over anything else. I considered his point and replied that the faith on which I rely is an individual's essential belief in and acknowledgement of God. However, it was my firm belief that individuals' expressions of their faith had helped and saved (and continue to help and save) many times more lives than were hurt and lost in conflicts that were wrongly described as motivated by faith. We ended up not agreeing.

It is my firm belief that successful managers need to have faith. Faith is the first necessary ingredient for this journey we all must take.

That faith is in the soul of the successful manager and it is that manager's own personal light. That light illuminates the manager's authentic self. It is **". . . this precious treasure – this light and power that now shine within us . . ."** (*2 Corinthians 4:7*). It guides the manager throughout the workday, during interactions and in decision making. It is the light in the open door that makes colleagues comfortable to come in and talk. It is the light of the manager's credibility. *It is the light of conscience.* It is the essence of the manager's spirit and humanity. While it may seem easy to put a cover over it, it takes an awful lot of effort to extinguish that light.

Think about people who give deathbed confessions and ask for forgiveness at their final hour. It would seem that at that point in a life, a confession wouldn't mean much to the confessor, after all he or she is checking out, right? *I guess they do it because they want to check out with the light on, not off.*

For some people, that light is visible with the human eye. Some thirty-five years ago, I had the privilege of meeting Mother Theresa at a church in the South Bronx - me and 300 other privileged people. She came to speak at the opening of one of her missions in New York City. Sitting in a pew in the back of the church, I stared at this tiny, short figure of a person dressed in white standing in front of the altar, surrounded by dozens of taller, bigger figures. Mother Theresa, however, was the only figure that was shining. Yes she was glowing, literally. It wasn't because there was a spotlight on her: this was a poor and simple church in a devastated neighborhood, it didn't have any spotlights. And at that time, unlike now, my vision was certified 20/20. Was I imagining this singular glow? My wife nudged me and asked, "Do you see it?" "The glow around Mother Theresa?" I asked in reply. "Yeah, that glow," she responded. We both turned to our friend who had accompanied us. Even though there were tears streaming down our friend's face, she could see it too. It was a powerful light, even more so when Mother Theresa insisted upon greeting and blessing each person present that day, as we filed out the door one at a time. Face to face, with Mother Theresa grasping my hand and saying, **"God bless you,"** the light from her was dazzling.

Listen to this one finding:

". . . 'A Spiritual Audit of Corporate America,' published in October (1999) by Jossey-Bass, found that employees who work for organizations they consider to be spiritual are less fearful, less likely to compromise their values, and more able to throw themselves into their jobs."

Isn't that the organization you want to build and represent? Isn't that the employee and manager you want to be?

This essential faith requires us as managers to believe in and demonstrate compassion for one another. I remind myself daily to practice compassion and to be a compassionate example, especially for my colleagues and my children. I admit to lapses in this regard but I catch myself quickly because I realize that my faith cannot be real without compassion as its expression.

The Logic of Compassion

There are times when I have been in disagreement or angry with a colleague or friend and I have found myself steaming inside to "get back" at that person! I admit it, I'm not perfect and I bet you've had similar thoughts in these situations as well. But I let those thoughts evaporate as I cool off that steam and my faith counters by listening to the logic of compassion.

This logical compassion isn't about inaction or surrender – it's about compassionate action that is motivated by my self respect. Instead of telling myself to "not sink to *someone else's* level," I am aware that I don't want to sink below *my own* standards and values. I make that choice, comparing the expression of me to my authentic self. Logical compassion requires that I respect myself; acknowledge and utilize the ambiguities of each situation; look long term at the consequences of my responses; and show respect for the person with whom I'm in disagreement. *Have anger, false pride, some other issue, or inattention prevented me from listening to the other person and responding, with an open heart?*

These considerations don't mean that sometimes my response won't be seen by the other person as negative and unwanted. Being faithful to myself and to what I believe, I use my leadership tools guided by logical compassion to respond appropriately, including with an honest criticism, a redress, a discipline or a termination. *These responses are done with openness, fairness, honesty and respect.*

The Light Shines Through

A number of times in my work life I've had to terminate the employment of colleagues, almost always in one on one situations, not mass layoffs. In a number of these situations, some time later I've come across these individuals again and they've told me two things.

1. Thank you for the respectful way in which you treated me during a difficult time.

2. Being fired turned out to be a blessing in disguise; I just couldn't see that at the time.

Surprising? It still is to me but it's true. It really isn't about what you need to do (unless you will be violating your own humanity) as much as it is about how you are motivated to do it. *When you take your lead from within yourself, from the light of your faith, even the most difficult management decisions will be morally clear and practically sound.*

Four times so far in my life I've been directed to end the employment of colleagues who had become my personal friends. I will tell you upfront that all remained my personal friends. My experience with one in particular, Wayne, is an abiding lesson for me.

Wayne and I became instant friends during my first two months in a new company. Wayne led one of the company's expanding product areas and I was the human resource leader. We met at a staff meeting and I was taken by Wayne's natural charm and his openness. Wayne hailed from Texas and his smooth, considered style of speech told me he was a proud son of that great state. If you met him, you'd like him – he just had a naturally likable personality. When he and I struck up a conversation, I realized there was a lot more to him than just charm. His insight about the people with whom he worked was on target. He was grounded securely in a set of personal values that respected each person as an individual and an equal.

At the heart of his values was his commitment as a born again Christian. He didn't announce it or flaunt it, he lived it. At a point in our relationship when we talked about faith, Wayne said simply, **"I'm a Christian, born again and that's how I live my life."**

Soon after we met, I began asking Wayne to keep his eyes and ears open for specific issues in the various company offices to which he traveled regularly. I knew that not only would he be able to hear what was on folks' minds in the company, but he was also trusted by every one of our colleagues.

For three years Wayne served the company, giving all of his efforts to try to right-size a problem product. Further complicating his work was a convoluted profit and loss system that hid inefficiencies and shifted losses so that some products looked to be better performers than they really were at the expense of other products' performance. I watched Wayne work through these roadblocks. He never lost his self respect, his faith or his compassion. It would have been easy, almost understandable, if he had blamed others for the problems he encountered and the battles he had to fight. He didn't.

At the end of his tenure, Wayne's managers decided he wasn't the person they wanted to continue leading the product. They wanted a different approach. I was directed to relieve Wayne of his command, with the help of the chief operating officer. Wayne was traveling to my office for a meeting and I discussed with the COO how we would break the news of his firing to Wayne. We agreed that we respected him too much to make him travel all the way from Texas to the east coast to be fired and turned back around afterward. We reached him on his cellphone and told him the news. I said, "Wayne, you really don't need to come here for a day so that we can fire you. Do you want to stay home and be with your family?"

Wayne responded, "Tony, thank you. I'm going to come to you. This is a difficult time and you and (the COO) may need me to help you through it."

I'd say I was a bit taken aback by his words. We need him to help us through this!? He was the one being fired. But Wayne didn't approach it that way. He knew we were anguished to have to do this and his concern was for us. The three of us met the next day and discussed the details. At the end of the termination meeting, Wayne asked us, "Are you fellas okay? I know this is hard on you guys and I want you to know I respect both of you. This doesn't affect our friendship." I thought I would be consoling him but it turned out Wayne was comforting me.

Being fired didn't dim Wayne's inner light. *If anything, it shone more brightly.* Wayne became a successful senior manager in a company

14

in Texas, blessed to be able to work in a respectful environment that utilized his talents and to be close to his strong and faithful family, for which he gave thanks.

You and I choose how we live our lives. More properly, we make hundreds of small choices each day that add up to the sum of our lives. In baseball an inch either way means a hit or an out. In football an inch can mean first down or punt. Everything we need to help us make the right choices and go those inches in our journeys successfully, we already possess.

Our most important choice is how we are going to use all of the best within us to achieve and sustain success.

Lesson:

"There is a destiny that makes us sisters and brothers. None of us goes his way alone. All that we send into the lives of others comes back into our own." Alicia Appleman-Jurman, Holocaust survivor and author of *Alicia, My Story*

Chapter Two

"What I'm saying is . . ."

The journey begins with people.

No matter what the topic of discussion, no matter what is being debated, analyzed, preached or legislated, the starting point is people. As a manager, your first duty is to manage people.

Your highest duty as a manager is to lead people.

This first duty has a number of assigned tasks – to listen, to teach, to understand, to monitor, to correct, to develop, to approve, to build a team. There are several good and profitable reasons why you accept this duty and perform these tasks – it's the job for which you are paid, it's your profession in which you take pride, you enjoy getting the job done right, your success and your team's success help grow the organization. And there is something inside of you that says being the leader of a successful group of people is satisfying and challenging, like being the head of a family.

You have one enormous advantage in leading the people on your team. You are a human being too. Although the blur of business ("Did we get that freight out to JFK yet???") may obscure this simple fact, you share all the same sets of emotions, needs, fears, and desires as your people. You may not show it at work but you laugh, cry and have doubts in the same natural ways that they do. And your basic needs for self-preservation, respect, recognition, discipline, nourishment, comfort and the rest are the same also.

These facts are so elemental that they probably seem simplistic as you read them.

Are they?

When did you last consider the straightforward humanity you share with everyone with whom you work everyday? When you look at the people on your team, do you see the individuals or do you see what you think of each of them? What do they see looking at you - the manager who knows, listens and cares about each of them or the face of someone who comes to work with the ultimate goal of leaving it behind as quickly as possible?

The one thing that happens every workday is you enter and leave your workplace as an individual person, a human being, no matter what else occurs in the intervening time. The same happens to everyone around you. Is your goal to be as successful a human being as you can be at work every day?

Let's Talk About That

For over thirty-five years I have been studying people at work, including studying my own behavior. Although my resume shows that I've held a number of different positions, Urban Planner, Management Analyst, Corruption Investigator, Deputy Mayor, Human Resources Vice President, and Human Resources Consultant, what all these positions have in common is my observing, listening, analyzing and reflecting on the subject of how and why do people behave at work.

During college, I worked as a maintenance person and administrative assistant for a real estate firm in Brooklyn Heights, NY. My boss was Ken Boss. That was his name, no fooling! He would say with a smile, "I was born to be a boss."

He was an attorney, a real estate investor, a collector of everything, an artist, a writer, a candidate for public office, a gadfly, a political activist, a landlord, and a surrogate uncle to me. In short, he was an amazing, confusing, dynamic bundle of human energy. Yes, I never knew anyone like him, before or since. He had all the money he would ever need, and then some, but if he saw a toaster on top of a garbage can, he would take it. "If you saw a five-dollar bill on the ground," he asked me, "would you take it?" Of course. "Well this toaster isn't broken, the person just doesn't want it anymore and it's worth at least five-dollars!"

Oh, he had a rule about collecting. "I don't pick garbage. I only take what's on top!"

Don't laugh, he found the original printer's galleys for a book by a well known author who lived in the neighborhood, with the author's handwritten corrections and comments. I think that piece eventually brought a tidy sum at auction. The Boss home, a magnificent brownstone on one of the finest streets in Brooklyn Heights, had a TV in every room except the baths. I don't think Ken bought any of those sets.

He either used or gave to others, including many of his tenants, the refurbished toasters and TV sets and other disjecta he collected. He was a self-proclaimed, card-carrying Socialist. He didn't do too shabbily as a capitalist, either.

I painted apartments, cleaned hallways and fixed minor leaks in his buildings during my last 18 months of college. Upon graduation from college, I worked in his office.

Thus began my career of studying people. You learn a lot by listening to tenants complain to their landlord. I learned a lot by watching Ken hold the phone away from his ear while one more tenant confirmed that the discoloration in the porcelain of his toilet bowl required the installation of a whole new one. Every two minutes or so Ken would put the receiver back to his ear and say, "I see."

Well, he didn't see; he was on the phone. And he didn't seem to hear because he didn't seem to be listening. And he didn't seem to want to hear. But when the call was concluded, I was dispatched to carefully paint over the discoloration and make another tenant satisfied.

Okay, maybe this wasn't the height of customer service but in its way it worked. The tenant had a chance to vent without being interrupted. Once Ken knew what the tenant wanted, a suitable, cost-effective solution was devised and implemented. The tenant saw a response that usually was more than acceptable.

The Big Lessons

One of the most important elements in dealing with people successfully, if not the most important element, is *Listening.* *So the next time someone at work states, "What I'm saying is . . ." you should be able to respond honestly, "I hear you. I know what you're saying. I'm listening to you."*

This book has two starting points in my life, both of which intimately involved my ability to listen.

The first was when I was asked by the Mayor of the City of Yonkers, NY to become his Deputy. For eight months I was in charge of Yonkers' municipal corruption investigations. In Yonkers, that made me part of a growth industry; Yonkers was one of, if not the most, corrupt cities in America.

Loan sharking on government property. Selling public offices. Steering government services to unqualified friends and benefactors. Yonkers had it all. Every time the politically driven investigators from outside the City came in to look at my conduct, I was cleared. In fact, years later I met one of the most vociferous critics of the administration in which I served, at a reception in Albany, NY. She took my hand, smiled and said she knew me from somewhere. I replied, "You investigated me three times and three times found me clean!" She laughed, gave me a kiss on the cheek and said, "Let's be friends."

Well, after eight months of doing what I enjoyed, solving complex problems and bringing service back to the residents, the Mayor asked me to be his Deputy. It wasn't what I signed on for but when a mayor asks you to serve, you serve. For over two years, I served the people of Yonkers as their Deputy Mayor.

On the first day I assumed that office, the Public Works Commissioner resigned. He assured me it wasn't my fault, he just couldn't work with the rest of the administration. I thanked him for his service and he warned me, "Beware of who you trust." This would be difficult for me to do because I have a tendency to be open and trusting in my dealings with everyone.

The Public Works Department, or "the DPW" as Yonkers citizens called it, was a customer service mess. Streets weren't cleaned regularly, only the ones in the districts of powerful council members. Recycling meant emptying the recyclables into the backs of garbage trucks full of garbage. Snow removal didn't happen in some parts of town. Autumn leaf pickups from one part of town often found their way to huge rotting piles in front of residents' homes on the other side of the City.

The responsibility to fix this was mine. I was accountable to the residents, including the Mayor and there were 150,000 pairs of eyes on my performance. But I wasn't alone in this job. I had an army of Teamsters who picked up the trash, cleaned the streets, plowed the snow, removed the leaves, and recycled the recyclables. They were a group of several hundred men and women, who had endured years of political manipulation, from all sides, and tried their best to do their jobs.

On my first day on tour of the City with Al, the lead DPW Enforcement Agent, he turned to me and said, "Someone wants to meet you." He drove us to an old City building and took me to a basement office. It was as if we were in an old movie about a tough town and the new sheriff was going to be ambushed.

Sitting in the basement office was the boss of the Teamsters local. I'll call him Tony Beef. He wasn't a large person, physically. In fact, he had fought and beaten cancer more than once so his voice was a deep growl with a hint of gravel in the delivery.

"Tony Shaw. I wanted to meet you. I hate your boss, the (bleeping) Mayor! I'm going to close the doors at City Hall after I kick him out! But you, I've heard good things about. Are you going to be fair to my men?" Word for word, this is what he said.

I responded, "It's unfortunate you hate the Mayor. I love him and I'm loyal to him. I plan to stay in City Hall for another term with him. I've heard a lot about you. Not all good but you are the head of the union and I respect that. I'll be fair; will you be honest with me?"

"I'll be honest. Treat my men fairly and I'll watch your back. But you watch your front, not because of me but there are plenty of people on your team who will screw you." Except he didn't say "screw."

We shook hands. I admit my knees were shaking too. I knew he was right. There were members of the administration who didn't agree with my approach to the Teamsters and wanted me to fail. If I was fair in dealing with our workers, Mr. Beef would represent them and be fair in return dealing with me. That meant if I caught someone not doing his or her duty properly, I would manage that by the union contract and discipline accordingly, up to and including firing. Tony Beef had the legal duty to represent the union members. I had the legal and moral duty to ensure the City delivered its services. I said to him, "I'm told the union manages the DPW. If it's true, it's over. I manage the DPW."

He looked at me and smiled. "If the union does run the DPW it's only because you people haven't managed it like you should!" We both laughed because he was right. The duty to manage fully and properly is management's alone. Says so in every union contract I've ever read. Usually management hasn't read the contract and that's where the problem starts.

After meeting Tony, I decided I had only one strategy to do my duty for the City and the Mayor who placed their trust in me: **Listen**.

I went out to the garages, work sites, lunchrooms, and anywhere else City workers gathered. I introduced myself and said "I'm here to listen to what you have to say. I never collected trash or plowed a snowy street in my life. You're the experts and you're also City residents. How can we do this better, quicker, cheaper?"

No one in my position had ever done this before – admit his ignorance, shut up and just listen. The response was some workers didn't know what to think, some didn't trust me, but some had waited for years to voice their ideas.

We plowed through six snow and ice storms my first winter. We weren't perfect, we were learning under fire (really under ice) but we were measurably much better than ever before. Neighborhoods where previously Mother Nature melted the snow before a City plow got there, finally saw snow removal equipment within hours of the storms. At a neighborhood meeting many months after that first winter, a woman stood up and said, "Deputy Mayor, we've never met but you had the streets around my children's school plowed right after I called your office. That never happened before. I just wanted to say thanks." That made my job worthwhile.

Why were we better? Because we put managers in the streets, on the plows with the workers and made them learn from each other. I rode with three great guys, long time union members, who taught me how to plow snow and remove ice. Their practical ideas contradicted many of my impressions about delivering these services but their ideas worked.

One more example: the City had never met its recycling target set by Westchester County. Never. Not even close. And the overtime budget for trash removal and recycling was out of control by about 150%! My solution was to ask the sanitation workers what were we doing wrong and how do we fix it. *You would think a worker wouldn't suggest ways to cut his or her own paycheck. You would be wrong.*

The workers told me three things. First, the overtime pay was blood money because they didn't want to haul refuse for 10 hours a day. Second, most of them had second jobs; some even took care of their kids. They wanted to leave work at a decent hour with the job done for the day. Third, if the City radically changed the trash removal and recycling pick up schedule, the job would get done, the recycling numbers would go up, and overtime would go down. This wasn't a consultant's recommendation. This was straight from the workers' mouths and hearts.

And it worked.

Recycling complaints went from ten a day to once a week. Designated pick up days saw all the recycling collected. No more commingling garbage and recyclables. The workday was eight hours. Overtime dropped to under 1%.

The local newspaper, leaping before it looked, reported the City had yet again missed its recycling goals. Then I showed them the County figures. Yonkers had not only met its goals but adding in leaf composting and recycling motor oil, Yonkers had surpassed its goals. The local paper had to print an op-ed column by me, quoting the County's official report that confirmed by the numbers that Yonkers had more than met the target.

There is one other lesson in listening that I experienced, leading me to write this book.

On April 1, 2003 at 8:00 PM, I was driving back to my home in Westchester from Darien, CT. I had worked late and then stopped at a friend's restaurant for dinner.

The road was wet from an early evening rain. The weather was turning cooler. I was driving my new SUV and I was stopped at a light on Route 22 in North White Plains, a road and an intersection I encountered going and coming every workday. As the light turned green, I put my foot on the gas to go up the short incline at the intersection.

The next three seconds were a blur – the SUV's wheels skidded on the slick roadway, then lifted up as the 3000 lb. vehicle hydroplaned and swerved out of control into the incoming lanes of traffic. I struggled to turn the steering wheel, only to become aware that it and I were no longer controlling the flying vehicle. I realized I was headed straight for a telephone pole that was once to my left but was now in front of me. I didn't have time to think I was going to die. My life didn't flash before my eyes – there wasn't enough time. A half-second before impact, the vehicle made a quarter-circle turn as the passenger side wrapped around the telephone pole.

As the safety glass sprayed around me, the steel frame of the vehicle pushed in and around, and the passenger side safety curtain deployed, I understood three things:

1. *There had been no oncoming traffic or I would have slammed my vehicle (at upwards of 90 mph) head-on into another speeding car or truck.*
2. *Anyone who had been sitting on the passenger side of my vehicle would have died instantly.*
3. *I was still alive, and unhurt, for a reason.*

My vehicle was totaled. I unbuckled myself, brushed some glass pellets from my hair and walked away from the vehicle. A police officer arrived at the scene and said, "You were the driver in that wreck? You're walking around? I don't believe it."

When I went to reclaim my belongings from the wreckage the next day at the junk yard, the woman behind the desk said to me, "You were in that car? And you're alive?"

I listened and learned that I am a fallible but resilient person and that the Creator isn't finished with me down here yet.

> **"I really cannot count all of the times God has saved me from my own idiocy and carelessness. I should not really be alive. To Him, my endless praise and thanks. Literally, I should have been dead or in prison a dozen times and He saved me. I don't know why, but I am grateful." Ben Stein, *Fleeting Beauty***

Amen.

So I'm writing this book to make a difference in your life and share my story with you. Every workday for over thirty years I've had the privilege of talking to managers about problems, usually their immediate challenges in the workplace. I've done a lot of listening and learning. *Often, the only thing another human being wants is for someone to just listen.*

One of my friends, Rich has been an in-house recruiter for Fortune 500 companies for over 20 years. He has worked for IBM, Stanley Tools and several other large, successful organizations. For a number of years he was the recruiter on my human resources team in the freight business.

A manager in one of his previous companies told him, "Every time I come into your office and tell you my problems, you always give me the right answer. And I always leave feeling so much better. Thanks."

These were heartwarming words except Rich reports that he almost never gave the manager an answer. He just listened. No advice. No readymade solutions. He just listened intently and with empathy because this manager was baring his soul about work. Now the manager didn't work for Rich and Rich didn't work for the manager. They worked for the same company but not in the same department.

Along On the Journey
This book is my conversation with you along our journey. In this format we can't be as interactive as in a face-to-face conversation but I've anticipated many of your workplace concerns so that we can talk. If you listen intently and with your heart as well as your mind, you can hear me listening to you. I'm not an MBA and this book isn't my graduate thesis. It's not filled with case studies or flowcharts. In this book I talk to you about human experience, yours, mine and many others'. *It is my belief that you already have the tools to be a more successful manager.* I can help you recognize and use them, as I have helped the managers with whom I've been privileged to work. Neither you nor I are mistake-proof managers. *But we are fellow human beings, eager to do well while doing some good along the way.*

What is a Best Practice?
Throughout this book I will be using this term. A best practice is a work method that has been observed and analyzed by professionals, that produces effective and efficient results consistently. In the workplace, everyone from the receptionist to the CEO uses best

practices – best practices are the ways we get our work done that time and trial have shown us give the best cost effective results, easily and quickest. Most of the time, we don't identify these methods as best practices and, significantly, we aren't sharing them within the organization so that all of our colleagues are using them across the board. Best practices help us put our faith in motion successfully.

Being a successful manager is not unlike being a successful parent. People want to be loved but they also want to be led. Being a good parent means having patience, listening with empathy, being authentic, and helping your children find the right answers – not being paternalistic! No two parents do it the same way but when it works, it's the best feeling in the world. And you learn something new each day!

We are all alive to make a difference in our own lives and the lives of others, especially those around us, our families, friends, colleagues, and the people we meet. *Managers have the responsibility to lead in making a difference.* As a manager, you have that purpose and that belonging in your workplace just like a parent has in a home. And that doesn't mean to look down on the people who report to you – it means honoring your humble sense of your self and your reason for going to work.

This is best said by the poet David Whyte who consults and counsels managers on work as **"a pilgrimage of identity,"**

"Soul has to do with the way a human being belongs to their world, their work, or their human community. When there is little sense of belonging, there is little sense of soul."

Jim Dowd, professor of organizational behavior at IMD in Lausanne Switzerland draws on Whyte's work and reminds us that management is **"not all about intellect; it's not all about mastering data . . . It's about bringing everything (you) have to work, so (you) can connect with others."**

You're reading this book; you've made a choice to listen, connect and explore your belonging in the work world, how you look at yourself, how you treat others and how you care for your soul. This is a practical step and a leap of faith in your own humanity. ***You and I choose to be who we are at work.*** Let's explore that choice together as we travel our paths.

Lesson:

"He who answers before listening – that is his folly and his shame." *Proverbs 18:13*

Chapter Three

You are the leader

One of my colleagues, a senior manager at a firm where I led human resources, sent the following e-mail:

"My managers and I have learned much from you over the years and our company has become a significantly more professional and effective place of business as a result of your contribution. Last night on the way home I was thinking about some of the many lessons learned from T(ony) S(haw):

1. **Walk softly and carry the right-sized stick**
2. **Listen more, talk less**
3. **Fairness trumps everything**
4. **Ethics are not unprofitable**
5. **Our human resources are all we have to offer at the end of the day**
6. **You can always grow, and you should always do so**
7. **Ethical choices are not tough to discern. They are (or should be) very clear.**
8. **Always lead by example**
9. **Respect everyone**
10. **Assume good intent, but document everything!"**

When I read this e-mail I was touched beyond words. I'm a fairly sentimental person to begin with but what touched me wasn't his praise (although I appreciated it). What really got to me was his ability to distill in ten neat phrases so many major elements of what I had been preaching for so many years. Like the Yonkers resident who stood up unsolicited to thank my office for plowing the snow, this colleague's thoughtful words let me know I had done some good.

The best managers are leaders and the best leaders are teachers, gifted folks who give something of themselves back to their colleagues. *When you are authentic in your relationships with yourself and others, and you give from your life experience, a lesson, a story, a gesture, an empathic ear, a kind word, an honest criticism, sympathy, support, appropriate discipline, you have given from your soul.*

My colleague's ten elements illustrate the qualities of a true leader.

How Do Leaders Behave?
Leaders have a wonderful combination of strength and compassion in their personalities. That's the *walk softly and carry the right-sized stick* element. Picture General Eisenhower and President Lincoln, leaders in times of crisis – neither one known for the loudest speeches or the flashiest behavior. Think of the graceful economy of Lincoln's *Gettysburg Address* and Eisenhower addressing the troops before D-Day. *Listen more, talk less*. Their physical appearances would be labeled less than movie star handsome. Both are remembered as incredibly strong and determined individuals whose words and actions made them giants.

Always lead by example. Both are also remembered for their immense compassion, demonstrated in adverse times, and their courage in the face of tremendous injustice. That's the fairness trumps everything, respect everyone and ethical choices elements.

I don't know whether leaders are born or made. I don't think it matters. *We all have the capacity to show leadership in a given circumstance.* As managers you are called on to lead every workday. As my colleague points out, near the top of the list of leadership qualities is Listening. His phrase **"Listen more, talk less"** is on point.

There is a certain calm, an even-ness and focus that surround a leader. When the situation seems to be deteriorating fast, the leader is the one with the clear head, steady voice and sure hand. Think of the best teachers you've had – they could bring order to a classroom full of students and hold your attention for 45 minutes without breaking a sweat. Listen to the novelist Shelby Foote describe this quality in General U. S. Grant:

"He had what they call 'four-o'clock-in-the-morning courage.' You could wake him up at four o'clock in the morning and tell him they had just turned his (troops') right flank and he would be as cool as a cucumber. He had an ability to concentrate."

For almost five years I worked for a CEO who was a Swiss national. I'll call him Franz. He had come to the U.S. more than 20 years ago to seek his freedom and fortune in the freight business. When I met him he was at the top of his game, having assumed the second spot in the senior management team of the world's largest air freight company. He reported to, at least on paper, Tomas the CEO who had hired me and to whom I reported.

Franz and I got to know each other as we worked together in the integration of his previous company with the company for which we now both worked. He told me that when he began managing his previous company, based in Washington State, his first friend in the business was the head of human resources, so he had an appreciation of what I did. Despite the fact he had a strong relationship with his human resources leader, at the beginning of the integration I was chosen to head human resources for the integrated company. Throughout the integration process Franz respected and cooperated with my human resources team, calling on us for special projects and advice.

Three months into the integration, Franz came into my office and closed the door. It was 8:30 AM. I was sitting at my desk and he stood in front of it.

"Tony, Tomas resigned this morning to go work for our competitor."

I found the words difficult to stomach. We had just gotten off the ground as a new company. So much uncertainty had been resolved and we were poised to move forward and grow. Tomas meant so much to the company, having become CEO after many years. Most of my colleagues had worked with him for a decade or more and all of us knew him as a charismatic leader.

My first response was to pick up a pen from my desk and hurl it across the room.

Calmly, Franz picked up the pen, placed it back on my desk and said, "Okay. You're the head of HR. I'm coming to you first. A lot of people are going to be unsettled by this news. The company is now my responsibility and I need your help." His voice was even. If my emotional reaction affected him in any way, it seemed as if he understood my sorrow, disappointment and anger. I understood what Tomas did, I was angry at him, I wished him well and I wanted my company to move ahead despite him, all at the same time. And Franz understood that as well. He probably didn't agree with all of my sentiments but he understood them in me.

Together Franz and I, with the General Counsel, worked to smooth the transition of Tomas' departure and Franz's assumption of the CEO position. Franz showed his leadership qualities in many ways. There was no midnight massacre of Tomas' close friends and relatives who occupied many key company positions. In fact, Franz approached all of them and asked them to stay because they were important to the company's continued success. Some stayed and many left to join Tomas at our competitor. Franz didn't have to say I was his HR head. He showed it by relying on my advice and the work of my team. Four months later, at the company's holiday party Franz asked me to sit at his table. His wife, whom I had not met previously, took my hand and said, "I'm happy to meet you. Franz was so happy when he learned you were staying as his HR head." Her words meant more to me than a raise.

Nine months pass to September 11, 2001. After an early morning doctor's appointment and listening to a CD in my car, I arrived at my office and was told by the receptionist that a plane had crashed into the World Trade Center accidentally. I was unnerved for two reasons; I hate to fly and for almost eight years I was in the Trade Center every work day.

I ran up the stairs past my office and into the boardroom where I knew the TV would be on. A handful of my colleagues, looking bewildered and frightened, watched as a second plane hit the Towers. Our perception of the situation changed immediately from accident to attack. Everyone, including me, began crying. Someone was doing this to us. Who do I know in the Towers? Our head of benefits commuted from New Jersey through the Towers train station. Had anyone heard from him? No. Are any of our people in the air today? Don't know offhand.

I gathered everyone in the boardroom as the terror played out on the screen in front of me and announced that anyone who wanted to go home could leave on administrative absence. Anyone who wanted to stay and work or watch the events on TV should stay. Anyone who needed to talk to someone should come to my office. I didn't know what else to do.

Franz flew all the time. Three out of five workdays he was in the air or about to board a plane. I didn't know where he was. I tried his cellphone number. No answer. I called his assistant. He's out of the office. I tried to think of what else to do. I couldn't come up with anything other than go back to the boardroom, watch the news and try to be a comfort for anyone in need.

As I watched the news, I remembered Franz telling me he once flew into Beirut during the civil war to collect an air freight debt. He got the check and flew back out the same day. I asked him if he was scared. "I felt better once the flight out took off!"

I couldn't figure out if he was fearless, crazy, determined or a bit of all three. But I knew he had four o'clock in the morning courage. What he did next confirmed it for me.

On September 13, 2001, Franz's management team met in the boardroom where so many of us had cried days before. In one of the most elegant and impressive displays of high level teamwork in the midst of a crisis I had ever seen, with Franz's guidance we coordinated efforts to support and reassure our employees, inform and assist our clients, and assess the damage 9/11 had done to our business. We also discussed ways our company could aid our country during this period. This was all done smoothly and effectively. In the coming weeks, our customers would praise us for our poise and efficiency. Our colleagues would thank us for our compassion.

Then Franz announced that all business travel by plane was suspended for the indefinite future. That meant domestic and international travel. This was from the man who flew into a civil war to collect a debt. I knew he would continue to fly (and he did) and I knew his bosses in Switzerland would not agree with the air travel ban. I asked Franz about this privately. "Whether they agree or not, I'm not letting my people risk this. We're Americans and our risk is greater. The bosses in Switzerland will have to understand."

I know Franz defied them because we didn't fly for three months and I took a beating from the Swiss HR managers for not flying to Europe for a meeting. But Franz backed me 100% and he backed his people 100%. In addition to the enormous emotional and spiritual toll on all of us, the company took a terrible financial beating because of these events. We went from a modest profit to losing tens of millions of dollars for the year. The company received no government assistance, while other U.S.-based freight companies did receive government aid, because our corporate leaders weren't American citizens. Ninety-eight percent of our U.S. employees were American citizens and they took a financial beating because of 9/11. None of this compared to our national tragedy. As Americans, we were stunned, angered and emotionally spent for many months well into the next year. *When we needed leadership, real 4:00 in the morning leadership, Franz provided it.*

I will never forget his example. He and I didn't always agree. We promised each other at the beginning of our relationship that we would disagree at times but be agreeable. We kept this promise. *Leadership and management are both an art and a science.* Lincoln ran through a number of generals before he picked Grant. Eisenhower's troops suffered dreadful losses before D-Day was successful. *You can always grow, and you should always do so.*

Learning From Erring

Leaders carry their own mantles of responsibility, in failure and in success. Rather than hiding from your mistakes and hiding from possibly making a mistake, your skills and your soul need the experience of mistakes to learn and grow. **"Resilient people view mistakes as experiences to learn from."** Managers need to see themselves and their teams honestly, not as Super- men or -women, but as imperfect human beings.

> **"There is nothing final about a mistake, except its being taken as final." Phyllis Bottome, English author (1884-1963)**

Apple Computer almost went into bankruptcy not so long ago. Harry Truman and U.S. Grant failed at every business venture they each tried in their lives prior to public service. It is not trite to remind ourselves that we all make mistakes because we all do, more frequently than we might wish or admit.

> **". . . if at the end of the day all you can say is, 'So-and-so made a mistake,' you haven't solved anything. Telling people to be careful is not effective. Humans are not reliable that way. Some are better than others, but nobody's perfect. You need a solution that's not about making people perfect." James Bagian, former astronaut and current Director of Patient Safety at the Veterans Administration**

I am reminded by a colleague that many people in the workplace put inordinate value in being liked by their colleagues. Not loved, liked. For managers this can lead to not dealing with problems for fear that someone may be disciplined or criticized, jeopardizing that person's positive image of the manager. Similarly, some managers are perceived by some colleagues as being too strong in their management approach because the managers' motivation is to go all out, without taking into account the more restrained nature of these colleagues. I've witnessed workplaces where female managers who are articulate and capable are perceived as being too assertive and challenging. Their self assurance is perceived as cockiness. Finally, I've experienced some behaviors by managers trying to be likeable, that defy any description of appropriate. When I asked one female manager why she talked about her love life with her staff, she replied that she was being friendly and attempting to open up conversation with her team!

In these circumstances, it is the manager's responsibility as the leader to check his or her own behavior and examine the motives. Do you want to be liked for who you are or respected for confronting problems directly? It is an unfortunate reality that some workplaces are not accustomed to women in management (or African-Americans, Jews, Sikhs, etc.). In this regard, the 21st century hasn't taken hold everywhere. Managers may need to do extra leadership work to discuss with and counsel employees (male and female) about the realities of equal opportunity, respect and the law. The support and assistance of human resources are mandatory in these circumstances. *You may need to examine your own reactions to employee pushback to make sure your response is solely professional and not personal.* Again, human resources must be used to help you deal with any of your own attendant personal issues, if they arise. Have you considered the work climate, the company's policies and your own sense of propriety before you include personal issues in any business discussion?

As managers our duty is to accept the human reality in ourselves and those who depend upon our leadership. With our colleagues we build teams and systems, provide support, and monitor performance to isolate and minimize the possibilities for error, catch mistakes at the beginning, and acknowledge and resolve them before they grow and spread. Just as importantly, we must be the leaders and the human examples of a work environment where we cooperate openly, listen and communicate constantly, and assist each other continually so that individual performances are the essential parts of a productive structure based on authenticity, honesty and fairness. *The leaders in this structure recognize, reward, support and discipline in a transparent and seamless management style that develops each person's potential and nourishes his or her spirit.*

I met Jeff at a seminar on Accountability. Jeff is a regional manager for one of the biggest retail chains in the world. He is responsible for the managers of several large stores in important markets in the Northeast, accounting for tens of millions of dollars in annual sales. Listen to what he told me about what guides his management thinking,

"My father taught me that it is far better and much more productive to want to work for someone, than to have to work for someone."

"Why Am I Here?"

A company for which I worked undertook yet another re-organization, this time in the computer operations division. After the high watermark period of Y2K, when computer technicians, programmers and managers were in demand at the best prices and terms, computer operations have contracted with layoffs, downsizing and job exporting. It has been a very swift and sometimes brutal process. It has been particularly tough on the computer folks whose general approach to work life is sometimes more insular and self-focused than professionals in other areas. Quirky, often followed by the words "but brilliant," might best describe many of the computer folks with whom I've worked.

This re-organization was happening rapidly, its details finalized only two days before being announced. My human resource team and I fought with the company's Swiss management and its German corporate head of HR for the approval to bring in executive coaches to help ease the spiritual and practical impact on those whose jobs were in jeopardy and those who worked along side them. We argued that the computer operations managers were most in need of professional coaching during this time because their colleagues would turn to them first for advice and assurance.

Can you imagine a 10:00 PM long distance telephone conversation between the corporate HR leader in Switzerland and me in which one of the hotly debated topics was whether the re-organization team had the right to ask American workers what were their ages, were they married and how many children did they have, so that European salaries could be calculated? The answer from my side for each inappropriate request was a firm and final "No."

Just a day before the announcement meeting with computer operations was to occur, I secured approval for executive coaches to be in place. It took a face-to-face impassioned plea by me over dinner with the corporate HR leader, in front of the management team of the executive coaching firm. Maybe it was my adamant position or the logic of my plan or he just wanted me to shut up but out of the blue he said "If you think this is that important to have, then we have it." When he left the table, the president of the coaching firm told me, "I don't know what you hit him with but he looks beaten to me. Congratulations." ***Our human resources are all we have to offer at the end of the day.***

On the day of the announcement meeting, the faces in the crowd were clouded with despair and resignation. Many looked downright hostile. However, I gave a lot of credit to the corporate computer operations managers who flew to America to present their re-organization plan at the meeting. They followed a script the executive coaches and I wrote for them.

They were straightforward and honest – no holding back details, no sugarcoating, and no hiding from the audience or from the truth. The only off-note was when the corporate human resources guy stood up and said, "Why am I here?" and he didn't seem to have a credible answer to his own question.

I could see the looks on the faces in the crowd. At the end of the presentation, I stood up and said these are the plans; we have given the details to you as soon as was possible because we know these are your lives we're talking about. "I promise that I will be involved and available for you. I personally guarantee that every right to which you are due by law, company policy, and morally because you are employees of this company, you will receive and I will fight for them." I then asked Joe Tomaselli, one of the senior executive coaches we provided for them that day, to say a few words.

Joe hadn't expected to be called on to speak at that time but he was (and is) a consummate professional. He came forward, stood in front of the audience and said

"I'm here to help you get through this time of major change. We all know this is not easy. I will help you by listening to your concerns and giving you advice. Why am I here? Because I've made every mistake in the book." *The audience's eyes widened in collective surprise.* "I've made mistakes that you might make and then some! And I've learned from those mistakes so that you don't have to make them to learn too."

He gained their trust in seven sentences because fairness trumps everything.

You Bring It With You
A leader's credibility is the core of his or her ability to manage successfully. It is truly said that all you take with you from one job to another is your reputation. Without your credibility, your other management tools are useless. Managers like Joe live authentic lives that confirm their credibility and speak their reputations instantly. *Leaders are both humble and bold.* By speaking and living from the essence of their lives **("I've made every mistake in the book")**, they relate to their colleagues immediately and their colleagues relate to and trust them.

> **"The lessons about a leader being both humble and bold cause me some thought. I've had too many examples of self-centered leadership." Dr. Terry Ebert, Managing Director, The Ayers Group**

My friend Peter, my first teacher in the freight business, told me, **"A true leader is willing to go out on a limb in pursuit of the truth."** Leadership and successful management are not timid pursuits. Managers face problems and conflicting situations constantly. Although performing as a team is the most spiritually rewarding work environment, the daily tasks required of managers include uncooperative people, unrealistic schedules and disagreements among and sometimes with colleagues that defy easy resolution. *The leader must be prepared ("Carry the right-sized stick") to first understand and then conquer these challenges.* There are many circumstances in which the manager's manager isn't going to accept anything other than a quick and sure answer.

No manager with whom I've ever worked expected me to predict the future; every manager with whom I've ever worked expected me to assist in planning for the future.

You are the leader in these situations. *Your first goal is to be aware of your own moral priorities, your values, what your role is in these circumstances and how you are approaching these problems.* The first place you look is within yourself. Ask, do I have a pre-existing prejudice about anyone or anything involved in this situation? What do I know about these people and circumstances and what don't I know? Where and to whom do I need to go to listen and develop a better understanding?

You practice the rule "Listen more, talk less." That means you pursue your open-ended questions (What can you tell me to help me understand this problem? How do you see this situation? What do you suggest we do to resolve this?) by hearing what each person has to say; by demonstrating with your attention span, facial expressions, body language, and follow up questions that what is being said is of value; and by respecting each viewpoint (especially the ones with which you might otherwise personally disagree). And although the workplace is assuredly not a democracy, it must be a place of fairness. *The significant feature of a fair environment is not majority rule; it is the minority's ability to speak safely and appropriately and be heard.*

Rather than being confused or overwhelmed by conflicting information, you are strengthened in your problem resolution and decisionmaking abilities by having a larger picture of what is involved. Remember the Teamsters who suggested ways to cut their overtime. I would have never arrived at that conclusion if I hadn't suspended my personal prejudices (Cost savings suggested by Teamsters!?). *Respect everyone.*

Instead of avoiding ambiguous information, welcome it. *One of the benefits of ambiguity is that by considering it, you make yourself think about the problem in more depth.* You know the management tendency to jump into a problem without taking the time to understand all the issues. Resist it. There are textures to problem situations that are revealed only when there is sufficient input. Do you want the quickest answer or the right answer in an appropriate time? Leaders appreciate Samuel Johnson's wisdom of two-hundred and thirty years ago, **"Knowledge is of two kinds. We know a subject ourselves, or we know where we can find information upon it."**

> **" . . . commitment to openness means we have to make an effort to listen to others, to integrate their perspectives where possible, and to tolerate differences as long as the differences are peaceful. Testing our beliefs in the crucible of others' perspectives will either make our beliefs stronger or create new intellectual alloys we never thought possible."** Max Borders, *Rational Mysticism for a Young Movement*

We haven't touched on that tenth leadership element, *"Assume good intent, but document everything,"* until now.

The legal and regulatory world in which we work requires us as managers to protect our colleagues, our organization and ourselves from the ugly consequences of charges of deliberate unfairness, unlawful prejudice and a disrespectful atmosphere at work. These charges, whether they are not formalized but only whispered, they are made in the organization's complaint process, or they are filed as legal actions, cost more than just managers' time to investigate and attorney's fees. They cost more than your potential personal liability that may be involved. *These charges destroy the workplace if left unchecked and they deteriorate the organization's credibility with both current employees and prospective hires and customers.* They undermine productivity directly.

You know that most work problems are people issues. You are the leader of an important group of people, your team. Where there is a problem or a situation that is building into a problem, you are responsible for knowing about it and resolving it. In recent decisions, the U.S. Supreme Court ruled that **". . . companies can be held liable for the illegal harassing behavior of supervisors even when top managers had no idea that it was going on and were not negligent in any way."**

41

The Court is saying that you as the manager, as the leader must be aware of and are responsible for what is happening around you, even when your colleagues don't tell you to your face.

This is part of the mantle of your leadership responsibility. You're not expected to be clairvoyant but you are required to listen. If there is whispering, you must hear it. When your colleagues are testy with one another, you must inquire why. When productivity slows, you seek out the human reasons. *Your people want to talk to you and they want you to listen – make that happen all the time because you don't have the time to not listen.*

When you are faced with a problem and you go through the steps to resolve it, nothing serves to protect all involved more than your documenting what you learn. A simple set of notes that are maintained properly are usually all that is needed. In a later chapter of this discussion, we will talk about documentation in more detail. So far as your leadership duties are concerned, you entrust your findings in any problem resolution instance to a documented format. While assuming good intent on the part of everyone involved in the information gathering and resolution process, you safeguard your involvement adequately through documentation.

Your agreement with your own manager is to take the right action in a reasonable time that finally resolves important issues and sets the foundation for lasting solutions. *Sometimes you have to stretch just beyond your normal reach to grasp the truth.* Your credibility and track record for bringing back the truth are the down payments on that agreement.

Our first set of management tools is the set with which we are born – our inherent humanity, our moral compass and our soul. As we grow and mature, these tools are honed by our experiences with parents, family, friends and the world outside of our homes and schools.

We learn how to recognize each tool and its utility in different situations. Life demonstrates how to adapt our approach to fit each situation successfully and make ethical choices.

When we are listening with open hearts and minds, we learn and carry that knowledge forward with us to face new situations. And we do this with enormous personal satisfaction, a satisfaction that comes from within.

Clara Knopfler survived the Nazi death camps with her mother. When she gives witness to her experiences now she relates the following piece of advice from her father,

"Always learn as much as you can because no one can take away what is in your head."

Her father meant not only book learning but also the learning gained through sometimes bitter experiences that test our humanity, values, ethics and spirit. This learning transcends graduate degrees and case studies. This learning is imprinted on your soul. Listen to it because it is the most human part of you, the part that knows right from wrong, decency from disrespect and how you want to treat and be treated by your colleagues. It is the opposite of selfishness.

The most fundamental part of your role as a leader is to use that learning to direct how you apply all of your tools to fulfill your managerial responsibilities. The author of the classic management text *"Built to Last: Successful Habits of Visionary Companies,"* Jim Collins concluded in a 2001 study of leadership published in the *Harvard Business Review* that the best leaders **"possess a paradoxical mixture of personal humility and professional will. They are timid and ferocious. Shy and fearless."** According to Collins, these leaders, whom he calls **"Level 5, great leaders,"** exhibit **"the virtue of chivalry."** They are self-effacing, generous of spirit and praise, committed to excellence and patient.

> **"There is no limit to what can be accomplished if it doesn't matter who gets the credit."**

The principle is very clear to me: a self-centered person cannot be truly successful either within or outside of the workplace.

I am reminded of my Uncle Harold. He was my mother's brother, one of five boys and two girls. At the start of World War II, all five of my maternal uncles volunteered for the military. Of the five, only four returned alive. My Uncle Harold re-upped and became a career soldier. He served at the Battle of the Bulge. He served during the Korean War. He gave his country over twenty years of service. When I was ten, in 1965, he returned to his mother's (my grandmother's) home, ending his military career as an officer. I have a vivid picture in my mind of him on that day: he wasn't tall but he stood ramrod straight. He wore his Army dress uniform – the brass buttons sparkled and his battle ribbons and medals were numerous. I admired how he looked in that uniform: I was too young to be aware of how proud he was of his country and how proud I was of him. To me, he was every inch a hero. But he said nothing of his service. He just took off that beautiful uniform and hung it neatly in a closet, never to wear it or refer to it again. I would sneak peeks at that crisp jacket and imagine how I would look in it. But he never talked to me about what he did and saw while wearing it. He just went about his business. To this day, when he is long gone to his reward, I cannot imagine him saluting himself, in public or in private, or using his military service to ask others to give him something or vote for him.

He was chivalrous in the most generous and self-effacing way – he gave to his country and to the men he led without either expecting or wanting praise and thanks. He had the inner, self-satisfaction of duty. **He led and lived by example.**

Lesson:

I can hear my beloved stepfather, watching me at age 11 trying to cook, "You're going too fast. Slow down and pay attention. You'll always burn your eggs like that." Sure enough, I didn't get it right until I lowered the heat, let the egg come to room temperature before I cracked it, waited until the grease was hot enough, and took my time to handle the pan and spatula properly. He could have said nothing and let me learn by trial and error. He could have taken over and fried the egg for me. He could have admonished me that I was about to burn down the house! What he did was give me a patient, non-judgmental lesson, in a knowing but not condescending voice. On my journey whenever I fry an egg, I think of his advice.

Chapter Four

Authenticity

The biblical scholars describe Abraham, the father of three major religions, as a person so welcoming to strangers that each of the four flaps on his tent were open, inviting in travelers from the north, east, south and west.

I'm struck by the fact that not only was Abraham's tent open to invite all in but, in the reverse direction, his life was open for all to see. Why would he keep all the doors open, if there were secrets to hide? or if he wasn't comfortable with himself? By keeping the tent open on all sides, Abraham was making the statement that he himself was open to scrutiny and experiencing whatever life would bring him. *I think Abraham is an early example of one who lived an authentic life.*

There is a principle in Jewish life called **Nahat ru'ah**, meaning repose of the soul. **Nahat ru'ah** speaks to your sense of inner peace but it is more than just that. Inner peace is a gift we can give to ourselves, to recognize our dignity as human beings, to be self-aware and self-respectful and to honor our importance in this life. It is when we have this gift that we can better understand and be compassionate for others and live more successfully. Dealing with others authentically requires we first maintain inner, personal authenticity. Shakespeare advised us that to be true to others, we needed to be true to ourselves first.

Authenticity Isn't Perfect
How do you understand yourself, your values and feelings, and that inner light of conscience and faith? Do you feel truly secure and comfortable with what you stand for and who you are? Are you practicing and living the traits of a leader? Do you listen to yourself and face yourself squarely? Authenticity requires us to examine our own motives and feelings so that we can deal with ourselves and others openly, using our management tools effectively. Joe Tomaselli, the executive coach who

admitted to making every mistake in the book, says that when managers **"better understand themselves, they can more fully realize personal capacities and achieve integrity in relationships."**

In their book "*The Power of Resilience: Achieving Balance, Confidence, and Personal Strength in Your Life*," Drs. Robert B. Brooks and Sam Goldstein report that an essential element in enhancing your decision-making and problem-solving skills is strengthening your self respect. Brooks and Goldstein explain that self respect and self acceptance mean seeing your own strong and weak points honestly, and relating your own imperfect humanity with the skills and imperfections of others. **People who accomplish this build immunity to the harmful effects of stress, as they face life's challenges with vigor.**

Recognizing, appreciating and working with our own imperfections are keys to successful management. When the Hubble Telescope was first launched by the U.S., after many years and billions of dollars of research and development, NASA discovered that the mission's scientists and managers had not taken into account the effect of the space environment on the curvature of the telescope's lens.

Once in space, Hubble couldn't see clearly. Instead of focusing on the excuses for this mistake, NASA decided to study the error, learn from it, and re-engineer Hubble in orbit. NASA decided learning from its mistake was far more productive than recriminations and self doubt. They invested their energy in developing a creative solution out of a mistake. A shuttle crew docked with Hubble and repaired the lens in space. Hubble can now see 10.5 billion light years into the past. *Authentic managers produce results out of mistakes.*

If you believe you cannot, must not, will not make a mistake, you are not being authentic.

"True authenticity is the lack of perfection." Architect Gil Schafer

I have a valued friend who is an accomplished researcher and consultant on the applications of motivation in successful management. His advice and help have been unerringly on target and important for me. We first encountered each other by telephone, him calling my office for assistance with an animal welfare issue. When he wasn't treated professionally by the person on my team who answered the call, he asked to be directed to the manager, me. I don't remember even being given his name. I did, however, listen to his issue and his complaint, resolve the former and have the staffer who mismanaged his call, call him back and apologize for the latter. This took probably 15 minutes during the particular workday some fifteen years ago. The problem was solved.

Several years ago at a human resources conference, I received an invitation for dinner with one of the consultants presenting his expertise and products to the attendees. When I arrived for dinner, the table was set for two places. I waited five minutes and a smiling, diminutive man approached to shake my hand and be seated. He introduced himself and although I recognized his name from my management studies in college, nothing else about him was familiar. He then reminded me that he was the caller whose animal welfare issue I was able to resolve so quickly. I honestly didn't remember the incident but when he related that I had directed one of my team members to call him back to apologize, I knew his story was true. He then commented, "I invited you to dinner because I saw your name on the conference list and I wanted to say thank you for helping me." This was an unnecessary thank-you after so many years – but it was necessary for him because of who he was as an authentic person. During and after dinner, he didn't talk about his product. We enjoyed a great meal and greater fellowship learning about each other.

The philanthropist Laurance Rockefeller was eulogized as a person who taught great lessons, "by simply being himself every day of his life."

Authentic people listen with open hearts, maintain relationships, have a healthy sense of humor, keep their commitments and share who they are with others to establish bonds of mutual respect and interdependence. *We ask ourselves, "How do I use my own experiences and the experiences of others to better understand my colleagues?"* We have faith in ourselves and in the need to live and work with others to be successful. We accept and honor our own abilities and limitations, and those of others. We draw out the wisdom of our colleagues to augment our own ideas in solving problems.

We see life as a set of challenges and as a rewarding journey in which we have the chance to experience and appreciate the lives of others, as well as our own lives. *Authentic people aren't perfect – they strive to live their lives as the fullest expressions of their humanity, by being the best of who they truly are.*

Of the people with whom we work each day, many are authentic colleagues, bringing their true selves to their assignments. Dealing with them on a one to one and a team basis is efficient, productive and rewarding. With no hidden agendas or unspoken problems, most tasks are managed smoothly to completion. When problems arise, they manage ambiguous aspects and conflicting information with openness and the acceptance that out of ambiguity can develop lasting solutions. Authentic colleagues are the team members you cherish; they are the co-workers to whom the organization always turns when dedicated efforts are needed to perform critical tasks. As their managers, we establish a work environment and culture in which they can make suggestions, take reasonable chances, make and resolve mistakes, and succeed without fear.

A Jewish sage, Rabbi Nahman remarked, "The entire world is a narrow bridge; the essence is not to fear (*Likkutei Maharan 2:28*)." A significant part of our duty of support as authentic managers is to build that safe environment for our team.

You and I encounter a number of other colleagues who display other than authentic personalities and behaviors. Some people come to work unmotivated and uninvolved. They're there because they are given a regular paycheck. Their interest level is minimal. They do what they are directed to do, barely.

There is a remarkable difference between being at work and working.

One of our roles as managers is to understand and accept that not everyone is a proper fit for every organization or situation. As we discussed in the first chapter, an appropriate parting of the ways can benefit both parties. Instead, we need to talk about those colleagues whose inauthenticity is a roadblock to your management success. Lies and deceit are also present in the workplace and we have to deal with them.

The Liar Among Us
Which significant inauthentic character trait is more destructive in the workplace, lying or deceit? The index of the *New International Version of the Bible* lists the citations in the text for lying and deceit and their respective derivatives (lie, liar, deception, deceiving, etc.). According to the editors of the Bible, deceit tops lying in mentions 75 times to 43 times. Why?

Lying is usually an isolated situational act. Most of us are not habitual liars, weaving a path of untruth to cover our actions and decisions until we ourselves can't distinguish what is and isn't true. Lying at work occurs most often when we don't believe we can face up to a situation. And lies usually unravel in the hands of their perpetrators because for all of our other life skills, most of us aren't practiced liars. The most common results of a lie are discovery and embarrassment for the liar. To paraphrase Shakespeare, the lie usually explodes underneath the liar. The resulting humiliation is awful enough to limit our practice of this inauthentic trait.

Our jobs as managers are to understand how disastrous a reputation as a liar is to careers and success, set a truthful example for our team, and discipline and coach team members who lie. The few times in my management career when I have caught a colleague in a lie, I've taken that person aside and asked him or her to rethink and restate the position. In over 99% of these cases, my verbal warning has been sufficient to put an end to the behavior.

But you and I both know a tiny minority of the people with whom we have worked over the years who go well beyond the situational lie. I've managed two persistent liars. I'll call the first one Telephony. Telephony wasn't just a liar; he was deceitful. He was, as with many habitual liars, not a teller of big lies. Telephony practiced deceit by the margins.

Telephony was the purchasing manager for a large transportation company. He was part of the human resources team I was chosen to lead some years ago. (I've always been amazed by the inappropriate organization charts of some otherwise very sophisticated companies, that use the human resources function as the odds and ends bin. This company was one of them; I subsequently moved purchasing to its own department appropriately.) His personality was low key and quiet. My first impression of him was that he was probably a solid journeyman, capable, and under a lot of pressure to meet his colleagues' needs for supplies in short timeframes and at low costs.

My first hint that this initial assessment wasn't correct came when the benefits manager, a knowledgeable no-nonsense team player, came to me and said, "I know you don't appreciate a liar and neither do I. You will see for yourself, Telephony is a liar. Remember I warned you." This statement was face to face, it was definitive and it came from a person I knew was trustworthy and without pretense. I also knew that my benefits manager never gossiped; if he said something, he meant it and he would say it in public without equivocating. He was an authentic person.

Shortly after I began working with Telephony, I met with him and said, "We will get to know one another. Everyone on our team is an important part of making this company successful. My style is to be honest and expect honesty in return. At the start, we all have clean slates. I will prove my credibility to you by supporting you and telling you what the company needs from you. Please talk to me whenever you want. My door is open and I visit each office on a regular basis. Is there anything I can help you with now?" Telephony's response was, "Thank you. Good to meet you. I'm okay but very busy."

Within two weeks of my start, the e-mails from across the company began coming to me: we were told we would receive service but Telephony hasn't delivered; it's been two months and no labels as promised; the price we pay at Staples for forms is half what Telephony pays; etc. I gathered the e-mails and sat down with Telephony. "What's up?" I asked. "Oh, I'm a bit behind. Your predecessor had me overseeing construction projects and that took away from my purchasing duties." Okay, I told him, no more construction management, I will do that job. You stick to purchasing. Clear up your backlog. Call your internal customers who are complaining, hear them out, apologize for the inconvenience and deliver what is needed. If something can't be done in the next five days, tell your customer the truth and set a firm delivery date in the very near future. If you need my assistance, I'll help but the responsibility is yours to resolve all of these complaint situations. I will check with you before the end of the week. Okay?

His response was, "Thanks for taking the construction off my back. I'll get the rest done."

In two days Telephony called me from the road early one morning. "Hello. My car just caught fire on I-95. It's a mess. I can't make it in today." I listened to not only what he was saying but how he was saying it. It had the ring of untruth. When I saw him park his car the next morning, the vehicle was unmarked. Not the biggest lie in the history of employment but a marginal one, done to cover a reason for a day off. Maybe he did have a small engine fire. Maybe it was a fender bender. What was more important than the behavior was the motive - to cut a corner off the truth to abet his own comfort. Deceit by the margins.

In the next weeks, Telephony lied about almost every aspect of this work life. He told so many lies that it wasn't until after he left the company that most of them were revealed. He lied about his wife's medical condition to gain sympathy when he knew his days in the position were numbered. He lied about where he was during the workday: just prior to his termination, I discovered that he was using a small mailroom in one of the company's locations to hide out for hours at a time. He lied about paying bills, processing invoices, talking with vendors, ordering supplies and everything else. His deceit was overwhelming and also pathetic. On different occasions when I was close to uncovering another one of his lies, I offered him help in the form of an employee assistance program. He refused. Think of the tremendous effort he put into concocting his web of deceit, all for nothing.

The remainder of Telephony's tenure on the team went swiftly downhill. In a month he terminated his employment by not following through on ordering a wreath for the funeral of a colleague's father. After assuring me that the wreath was ordered (although the intended recipient told me tearfully she never saw it), he then said the florist hadn't delivered it. This was followed up with his claim that he wouldn't use that florist again because of their mistake. I called the florist and was told our company was a special customer. Their records showed no order for a wreath. I called Telephony into my office, closed the door and informed him that his course of lies amounted to a trail of deception that could not be tolerated by either the company or me. He protested his innocence even after I showed him the documentation from the florist. He vowed to go directly to the florist and bring back proof that he wasn't lying. I never heard from him again.

Regrettably, one of the best (or worst) examples of a practioner of deceit by the margins is a certain former politician. His public responses and testimony were full of deceits and intentional confusions that added up to a determined course of deception to save his own reputation, in plain sight of the American people. And it didn't work.

If you asked him, for example, if he had been unfaithful to his wife, his immediate response would be "No, I never had relations with (the other) woman." Behind that response, however, would be his peculiar line of marginal deceits.

It depends on what your definition of "is," is.

Why not wait until I'm caught to tell the truth.

Do you know this person? Had he simply said upfront, "I did it. I was wrong. I'm sorry. I'm going to apologize to my wife and child. Pray for me." he and the nation would have moved away from the scandal and forward into bigger and better things. His courage in being authentic and telling the truth in difficult circumstances would have been admired. No impeachment. No prolonged trial and national paralysis. But like Telephony, all his energy was wasted on the inauthenticity of deceit. Instead of trying to convince through authenticity, he favored seductive deceit. He could be deceptive from his hat to his shoes. Ben Franklin said sagely, **"Half a truth is often a great lie."**

An authentic person can convey honesty in seven sentences, or less. A deceitful person can write 900 pages and still cut corners with the truth.

It Does Come Back Around
Authentic people understand and live according to their faith that there is a very direct link between the way they act and what happens in their lives. Cause and effect travel in greater concentric circles than we can see and experience immediately. Various terms are used to describe this, circumstances and life returning to you what you put into them. There is the Hindu concept of ***dharma*** in which we are all part of a cycle of birth and rebirth, trying to not make the same mistakes that sentence us to be stuck in this cycle – because all actions have spiritual consequences (*karma*). **The scriptures advise us to cast our bread upon the waters and it will return to us multiplied (*Eccles. 11:1*) and that we will reap what we sow (*Galatians 6:7*).** In perhaps less lofty terms, we are warned to be careful about how we treat others as we go up the ladder of success because on the way down we will meet the same people. We know our reputations precede us. *Our authenticity is an expression of our conscience*.

Authentic people know that before they answer to anyone else, they answer to their authentic selves, to that inner source. Your authenticity monitors and applies the guidance needed to answer to yourself with honesty, reason and logical compassion along your journey. *Our Creator gave us a conscience to guide our motives and behaviors – our conscience is our moral Magnetic North.*

I once heard a priest describe our conscience as a measured measure: it only worked properly if it was calibrated correctly. He gave the example of a foot-long ruler that was manufactured by a standard of 11 inches instead of 12 – as it was used, it was assumed to be a measured foot but its measurements fell short by an inch! Thus, any wall it was used to measure was off-center, any window measured couldn't fit its opening. If our conscience is used consciously, we know when our application of it falls short: you've heard that little voice inside of you that says, you know this is wrong so why are you going to do it anyway? You manage and lead with this guidance. *Take care to ensure your relationships with yourself and your colleagues follow this guidance wisely and closely.*

The Long, Hard Look in the Mirror
Monsignor Edward Donovan of Mount Kisco, NY tells the story of ministering in a prison when he was a young priest. He asked a group of inmates about how they could be witnesses for their faith. There was a long, thoughtful silence. Prison life and the misdeeds that cause admission to prison weren't the easiest examples of being such a witness. One inmate spoke up and said, "To be a true witness, you have to be yourself." Not pretend. Not put up a wall or hide behind a façade. Not be someone else. **Through a life with lessons probably more painful than we can imagine, this inmate was talking about personal authenticity.** Many years later, Monsignor Donovan still told this story in his homily about making choices in our lives and faith.

> **"Laws change. Conscience doesn't." Spoken by the character of Sophie Scholl in the film *Sophie Scholl – The Final Days***

Organizations are composed of people, guided by the work environment and the culture nurtured by managers and leaders. Authentic managers and leaders encourage and maintain authentic teams and companies. *Leaders of companies need to take long hard looks into their inner mirrors to see who and what they are honestly.*

In the 1930s, 40s and 50s the Penn Central Railroad was considered a successful company. It met every prevailing definition of success: it was big, it made money, its stock performed well, and it paid dividends for 100 years straight. By the 60s and 70s, it was bust.

The leaders of the Penn Central didn't take the time to ask themselves what is this company and who are we. They took for granted that the Penn Central was a railroad, primarily a steam-driven railroad. In reality, the Penn Central was an enormous property-owning company and steam was on the way out. Unfortunately, as the railroad business started to give way to the airline, automobile and trucking businesses and electricity outpaced steam power, the leaders at the Penn Central were slow to recognize that the property they owned and managed was where their business focus belonged if they were to remain authentic. Every so often during their heyday, these leaders should have been asking themselves, "Who are we as a company? What should I be doing as a leader? What are my greatest strengths and weaknesses? Are we today where and what we were yesterday? What is our corporate motivation? What is our purpose?"

Maybe they could have asked an analyst. Probably, if they searched within the soul of their business, they would have found the answers, or enough ambiguous information to lead to better questions that led to better answers. But they didn't. There is no more Penn Central today, only the faded Penn Central logo on aging railroad cars in the ConRail fleet.

One of my colleagues was given the following list by his wife concerning what to do to have an authentic marriage partnership;

1. **Don't lie.**
2. **Do what you say you're going to do.**
3. **Take responsibility for your actions**.

It's a good checklist for personal authenticity in action.

Lesson:

Apple-Metro's CEO Zane Tankel takes a bold approach to reinforcing authenticity in the workplace. "When I ask (our employees) 'Who is the most important person who walks into the restaurant?' and they all go, 'the customer,' I say 'The customer is

not the most important person – but you are.' I don't want anyone to think we are a church or the Salvation Army but I say that because if they are happy, they will make our guests happy."

Chapter Five

Listening

The simplest and most perplexing feature of listening is that we believe and act on the belief that listening is an automatic process, a reflex. When a doorbell rings in our home, we think, "There is someone at the door who wants to come in so I'll get up, go to door and see who it is." When we pick up a book or a newspaper, we take a moment to consider do we want to read, what do we want to read, for how long do we want to read, where do we want to read, and similar considerations in preparation.

How much preparation do we do to listen? Do we even consider if we are listening effectively or what will be the outcomes of how we are listening? Listening is not a reflex. *It is a dedicated complex action that requires certain skills.* These skills need to be acknowledged, practiced and applied in order for us to be successful at listening.

You know that before a person says the first word to us in a conversation, we are already receiving communications from that person. We analyze and judge facial expression, body stance, proximity of the speaker to us, hand gestures, clothing, make-up, smell, previous opinions about him or her, other conversations related to the speaker, our own prior experiences with or about the speaker, the setting, our current emotional state, and much more – being reviewed in our mind within seconds before that first word is spoken.

And the person on the other side of the conversation is doing exactly the same. We begin listening to the words after applying all of this communication, without realizing that our listening is significantly modified and often hampered by a flood of judgments we've already made about the messenger and, subsequently, the message.

In those preliminary seconds, are we preparing ourselves to listen? Probably not.

Unlike answering the doorbell, we usually don't ask ourselves about our motives for how we will be perceiving, speaking and acting in a conversation before we listen. Our motives exist silently just underneath our conscious thoughts. We don't slow down long enough for self-analysis to take place, for us to be aware of ourselves on that secondary level below what we believe we are thinking about. We do, however, have the capacity and the ability to listen more effectively and authentically when we recognize and control what happens inside our mind before the conscious process of hearing occurs.

Listening at the Beginning
> **"How true is it that words are but the vague shadows of the volumes we mean. Little audible links, they are, chaining together great inaudible feelings and purposes." Theodore Dreiser, *Sister Carrie***

That is where the skill of listening begins. To better understand how we practice this skill, we need to appreciate our own "knowing about knowing," our objective knowledge in the moment of action about our own process of acting. This may be referred to as **metacognition** or **reflective practice**.

One of my Canadian sales colleagues once remarked, **"Some of the best selling I've ever done, I did with my mouth closed."** He meant not only that he listened before he spoke, but that he thought about his thought process as he listened. He made himself aware of where he was at in the moment of his listening encounter. He focused.

He reflected on what he was doing as he did it. By reflecting **while** doing, he gained profound "developmental insight." This is an intense and beneficial focus, within as well as outward. In the terms of a well known study of **reflective practice**, this is **"how professionals think in action."** I know friends to whom the word "focus" is a *mantra* to be consciously aware of what they are doing and what is occurring at any given time. We can choose to be awake, alive and fully aware in the moment rather than in a lull, daydreaming or sleepwalking. Have you ever felt that jolt of recognition that your mind and your body are in different places and have suddenly re-connected? I plead guilty.

But you don't have to be daydreaming to disconnect in the listening process – even when you think you're in the moment, you may be listening inadequately. Many times after a conversation, I've felt that I haven't heard everything that was said, including my own words, and how the speaker and I were conversing. I simply wasn't truly aware. The successful performance of the skill of listening demands that the listener (and the speaker) be in touch with his or her own inner listening process.

Think before you listen – be truly aware, be open to and consciously accept your role in the communication process and guide how you listen as you are listening. Be aware of why you may take an emotional stand or opinion about the speaker before the first word is spoken. Listening is intentional. Honest listening is reflective listening. ***Listen with an open heart, without prejudice and with the personal authenticity and self-respect to receive the speaker's full messages clearly.***

Listening includes hearing what is and isn't being said. According to one story, at the height of the Watergate scandal then President Nixon traveled west to visit the home state of Governor Dan Evans. After Governor Evans introduced the President, Nixon acknowledged the greeting by saying, "Thank you Governor Evidence." You know what was on his mind. The thought found a way out, embarrassingly. I am a firm believer that the truth will out and it is essential for managers to be ready to listen for it. Sometimes you need to listen for what the speaker isn't intending to say. At a large management conference I attended, the company leader stood up after the lunch break and announced (completely out of context), "I hate liars!" His audience was caught off guard because the topic of liars wasn't on the agenda. Now you should know, this leader was given to telling whoppers on a regular basis. Lying was a trait he just couldn't tolerate in anyone else!

In his study *"The Psychopathology of Everyday Life,"* Freud proposes that what may be overlooked in importance as slips of the tongue and forgotten names, is in fact the expression of repressed thoughts and unresolved issues. ***We can understand our colleagues' intended messages in greater depth by truly listening.***

What isn't being said is often expressed in volumes of silence; those long pauses in-between words, sentences, and questions and answers. My friends at Interact, the troupe of actors who worked with me on improving my listening and speaking skills in the workplace, taught me a priceless lesson in using silences for successful communication. Jack, the leader of the troupe, instructed me, **"The key to making silences work for you and not block communication, is to ensure the other person owns his or her silence. Then that person has to deal with it."**

As an example, he demonstrated that when one of my asked questions is met with silence, the best response on my part is to mentally count the length of the silence, allowing the silent party to take his or her time to gather thoughts and feelings about what I just said. For me to rush in on that colleague's silence, because I'm impatient or think I need an instantaneous reply, is to take ownership of the silence away from my colleague unfairly. Allow the silence to work. If after ten seconds (and that's a longer time than you think it is, count off ten seconds in your head and experience it!), the other party doesn't appear to be ready to respond, ask firmly but respectfully, "What are your thoughts?" This should open the door for the colleague to voice what was the essence of the silence.

Conversely, as the speaker I can use silence to emphasize a point or dramatize a question. I well remember the Baptist minister in whose church I grew up, Rev. Thomas, raising his voice to a fevered pitch on some point in Scripture, then falling silent as the congregation took in the gravity of what he had said. As we listened to his silence, we hungered for his next sentence but tantalizingly he made us wait. The effect was perfect, total undivided attention on the speaker.

Not listening has serious, damaging repercussions. In my professional experience so far, I have never seen a union organizing campaign in a previously non-union workplace that wasn't caused by local managers who didn't listen to their workers. Of the dozen instances in which I've had to represent management on the other side of a union organizing effort, I've uncovered one dozen situations in which local managers refused to listen in the workplace or simply didn't know how to listen. And not one of those dozen instances involved disputes about pay!

They involved workers who weren't treated like equals and human beings, abusive managers who were complained about with no results, uncaring and non-responsive bosses who hid in their offices rather than interact with colleagues, and similar work atrocities. People who come to work and feel that they aren't being listened to and aren't worthy of being listened to, are being brutalized. The union's organizing appeal is obvious; we will listen and protect you from management's brutalities. Had the local managers been listening, the unions would never have had a toehold. In offices and organizations where managers are authentic, aware, visible and listening, the union message usually does not thrive.

Being prepared to listen and listening with an open heart, empathic listening, will produce successful and rewarding results. You will hear and acknowledge subtle clues, references, contexts and images that reveal a deeper understanding and truth in the communication. You will see the speaker's story take shape and your appreciation of that story will extend beyond the words used. Your understanding of your role in the communication process will deepen as well.

One successful listening experience will replace many unsuccessful ones. Instead of being an unwitting victim of your own inadequate listening, you will be able to unveil aspects of any situation that will lead to managing your responsibilities more successfully. ***Reflective listeners become better critical thinkers.***

"(F)aith comes from listening . . ." *Romans 10:17*

The importance of listening is emphasized in the *Proverb*, **"Death and life are in the power of the tongue *(18:21)*."** And also in the ear and the mind.

Is Our Hearing Impaired?
In the mid-1980s I investigated and analyzed municipal corruption in the government of the City of New York (by the grace of God, I've always found myself in these jobs with limitless potential!). I was called into work one Saturday with the instruction that the Mayor's Office wanted me to accompany a squad of police, FBI agents and other investigators to seize the records of the Parking Violations Bureau, the "PVB." Previously, the Borough President of Queens had attempted suicide by stabbing himself in the chest.

The administration of New York Mayor Edward I. Koch was caught off-balance by a massive federal inquiry into the PVB, one of the city's cash cows. City revenue collected by the PVB from paid parking tickets was unaccounted for and lucrative contracts to automate the parking ticket process had been let to phony vendors.

I was part of the city's effort directed by the Mayor's Office to regain control of the situation by finding out what went wrong and why. This would turn out to be the biggest scandal in New York City history since the days of Boss Tweed.

When I arrived at the offices of the PVB, in the company of an FBI agent, I found a cavernous bullpen of a room, dark, gloomy and filled with desks and papers but not many people or partitioned cubicles. The few people who were there, other than the investigators, were managers who had custody of their work records but didn't want to be taken into custody themselves! The confusion and fear in the atmosphere were palpable.

The agent and I had been assigned specific areas to review and seize documents. By the end of the investigation, a year later, there were at least two huge storerooms filled with the boxes of records seized that Saturday.

One office to which we were assigned was tucked away in a singularly dark and isolated corner of the room. The manager sat at his messy desk, a middle-aged man with glasses, shaking visibly as we approached. He was in charge of the automated management information system, the system that reported the PVB's above-budget revenues year after year. I didn't know how tall this manager was because he remained seated, appearing to be fixed in his chair. He stammered as he spoke to us, answering our questions and complying with our requests (actually our demands) in a nervous but resigned voice.

The FBI agent and I got to the point of asking this manager the jackpot question, "How did things go wrong at the PVB?" The manager's answer still rings in my ears.

"I knew what they were doing was wrong. When we voted for the contracts, they wouldn't show us the prototypes or explain. You were sitting there with your boss – if he voted yes then you had to, too. He was sitting there with his boss! What do you think? I kept saying this was wrong but we reported larger and larger revenues every year, bigger than the budget targets. **Nobody would listen to me**."

Here was a government manager who looked intimidated but he had had the courage to question what he knew wasn't right. My subsequent investigations proved his statements to be true. He had spoken to others about his misgivings about the PVB's contracting process. He had been ignored. The perpetrators, who turned out to be the senior managers of the PVB and their political mentors, didn't even bother to shut him up or fire him. They stuck him in a corner, literally. *In their criminal conceit they knew no one would listen to him. They counted on a culture where no one listened. They stole millions of dollars based on that certainty and almost got away with it .*

Cultural differences effect skillful listening, frequently in subtle ways. Richard Hayes is a scholar at the Elijah Institute, an interfaith think tank in Israel. He brings the perspective of a former professor of Buddhist studies at Montreal's McGill University. Discussing communication difficulties between different faiths and cultures, Hayes comments, **"If** you look at the history of world religions, almost every tradition has a history of real grievances against another tradition. Sometimes people carry with them the historical burden of animosities of the past and retreat into positions of defensiveness instead of really listening to what other people are saying." Cultural barriers to listening can and do cross national boundaries as well.

I once received an employee newsletter from the head office of a global company for which I worked. The newsletter was intended to bring an employee community closer together around the world. To that end, it contained stories and photos of employee activities from every continent. This company did business in Antarctica, as well as everywhere else. One particular issue of this newsletter had a story about a vehicle road rally in Europe with accompanying photos, illustrating the participating employees and their vehicles. One of the captions explained that employees stood next to their "Jeeps" before the start of the race. The problem with the caption was the vehicles shown were Renaults, not "Jeeps." The story was in the English language newsletter, distributed to all American offices.

Being a loyal Jeep owner, I e-mailed the newsletter's editors and asked if the caption was incorrect. In response, an editor responded to say the caption was correct; the word "Jeep" was a "generic term" in Europe referring to any four-wheel drive vehicle. Not being totally satisfied with that response, I e-mailed in return that "Jeep," with a capitalized first letter was a trademark of Chrysler for the vehicles they produced and although "Jeep" may be generic in Europe, in the U.S. it identified only one brand. Not to be outdone, the editor responded that the newsletter was written (in English) in Germany, therefore the use of "Jeep" was appropriate!

My own prejudices in favor of the vehicle I owned and against being lectured by my foreign colleagues matched my colleagues' prejudices of blindly defending what they wrote and being offended about being corrected by an American, resulting in neither side listening to the other. Was my position right, technically? Yes. Were my colleagues right in assuming that their colloquialism was a correct usage in context? Yes.

Neither they nor I was attentive to the true substance of the conversation and to each other. By not listening to each other, by approaching this communication unfocused and with closed hearts, we failed to do our jobs successfully. We failed.

What was the correct answer to this problem? I should have suggested that the word "Jeep" be spelled with a small "j" and they should have volunteered to use that proper terminology in future U.S. editions.

Einstein said insanity was doing the same thing over and over, and expecting different results! In our journey, we find ourselves in similar situations time after time. How we approach each of these situations determines if we will move ahead, retreat or be stuck in neutral. Inadequate, incomplete listening will hold us back, with the same poor results invariably.

The Listening Practice
One of the most entertaining exercises to sharpen listening skills by observing a situation filled with decisionmaking on a life or death level, totally dependent on successful listening, is to watch the film *"Twelve Angry Men"* starring Henry Fonda and Lee J. Cobb. Ninety-five percent of the film's story takes place in a closed room where a jury of 12 decides the fate of a young man accused of murder.

The deliberations begin with a vote of 11 to 1 for conviction. As the story unfolds, the lone holdout for acquittal argues his side and tries to convince his fellow jurors, one or two at a time, that what they see as an easy decision is far more complicated. He challenges the truths held by his peers collectively and relies on the jurors' innate wisdom and ability to listen to motivate them to examine their opinions.

Watch this film and focus your attention on the interactions between the lead character and one of the other jurors - the blue collar worker with the baseball tickets, or the immigrant citizen, or the fussbudget who doesn't remove his suit jacket and never sweats (played memorably by E. G. Marshall), or the ad executive, or one of the others. *What is wonderfully enacted is how the lead character communicates with each person, listening with an open heart past that person's prejudices and disagreements to a place of common ground, and then building on that basis.* Because the film's events are confined to a closed room, the action is all talking and, most importantly, listening!

The film illustrates the vitality of each character's authenticity in the context of all the other characters and how this authenticity colors the characters' listening and communications abilities. The variety of personalities and styles portrayed rivals what we as managers see and deal with every workday.

We have the managerial responsibilities to listen successfully and effectively, to practice reflection, and to motivate our team to do the same. So much of the unsuccessful listening I've witnessed, been a part of, or caused myself has been a direct result of decisionmaking based on out of control ego and selfishness, rather than acting from personal authenticity and true leadership. *Remember, it is what motivates the behavior that is key in changing that behavior.*

> **"We fall into sin when we are ignorant of the motives beneath the desires. Consider this way of understanding personal sin: We sin, not because we are in touch with our desires but precisely because we are NOT in touch with them!"** *Catholic Update Guide to Vocations,* **Mary Carol Kendzia series editor**

The philosopher Thomas Merton described Adam's original sin as **"substitut(ing) self-assertion for self-realization . . ."** When Man overcame this sin of misplaced motive, he was **"once again able to drink from the inexhaustible spring of truth . . . hidden in the depths of man's own nature . . ."** The reflective listener who hears the real message clearly.

To develop empathic listening skills, practice reflection and ask yourself;

- Have I prepared myself to listen? I put my present work aside so that I just listen.

- Am I focused, aware in the moment and attentive? I want to hear what is said.

- What preconceptions, prejudices and inner messages do I bring to this conversation, even before it begins? I want to hear, not judge.

- Am I confident that I am going to think and listen first, not judge the message or try to solve the problem hastily? My body language is inviting.

- Am I prepared to accept the ambiguities that may present themselves in this conversation and utilize this information to broaden my own considerations? The speaker may indeed have new, different or conflicting information that is useful to me.

- If I disagree with the speaker's message, in whole or in part, do I understand clearly why I disagree? Even if I disagree, I want to truly listen to what is being said, not what I want to oppose or criticize.

- Is my disagreement logical or emotional? I may need to listen more and evaluate later.

- Am I pushing my own point instead of listening to understand the speaker's point? My point may be valid but the speaker's point may be useful.

- Am I treating both the speaker and myself with respect in this conversation? I wouldn't want to be treated disrespectfully while I'm speaking.

- Have my questions to the speaker been open-ended, inviting additional information? The answers to my questions are fully formed, informative and helpful.

- Have I allowed the other party to own his or her silences? Have I used my own silences effectively? I'm not rushing the speaker, whose pauses may reflect careful thought. I'm giving my listener space during my talk to understand the depth of what I'm saying.

- Have I given myself the opportunity to analyze the speaker's message honestly and carefully without frustrating that opportunity by perceiving my own viewpoint only? I paraphrase the speaker's statements to ensure I'm really hearing what is being said.

- Do I need to seek additional information after this conversation, and if so, where and from whom? There is probably more work to be done to get the facts and form a conclusion.

Successful listening with empathy does not mean passive acceptance of anything and everything being said. It means exactly the opposite – an honest, thoughtful, full and open intake and exchange of information. The listener doesn't have to either agree falsely with everything said or disrespect the speaker by not allowing everything to be heard. The emphatic listener communicates his or her own reactions and questions in a conversation to deepen the resulting understand by both him- or her- self and the speaker. *Asking open questions permits the listener to draw out the speaker's wisdom and contribution.*

Roadblocks
In my professional journey, I've met (and dealt with) a number of colleagues who present a particular puzzle – outwardly they are gregarious (often too much so), boastful and quick to comment and proclaim knowledge about almost everything. They can be humorous and intriguing but continued relationship with them over time reveals a sad reality: they actually have very low self-image, no self-realization, a reticence to admit weakness, and a thin veneer of braggadocio and chip-on-the-shoulder that covers a desperate need to be acknowledged and heard. Often they are the worst listeners – deep self-doubt preventing their acknowledging and hearing others. They have required my most intensive

efforts to motivate to be better listeners. *Teach listening by demonstrating true listening and reminding others to "please, just listen, thanks."*

Another roadblock we may face is technology that has given us so many seeming advancements, that are really impediments to effective communication. Cellphones, ipods, text messaging and ipads, among other innovations are everywhere. So much so that rather than assisting in the communication process, the presence of these elements can stand in its way. What is occurring with these technologies is most likely reaction, not communication. And we become conditioned to react, not listen.

> **"A face-to-face conversation between people is becoming less and less common as technology gradually becomes the more desirable form of human interaction. Genuine human communication, however, is not possible with a technological 'middleman.' " Gabriel Kates-Shaw, "*Reliance on Technology is Changing Human Society*"**

As a result we may tend more to hear what we wanted to hear, not what was being said, and be disconnected from **practicing reflective listening**. Be aware that often you may need to sum up a critical conversation at the conclusion or ask the other party to summarize what was discussed, to ensure you got across the intended message or conveyed the intended information effectively. *Trust but verify.*

> *At one of my clients the decision was made to separate the two top managers in the administrative area. The president spoke to both of them individually and from a script told each of them the exact same message – they should stay two more days, transition their work and then leave on severance. Nothing more, nothing less. Immediately afterward, when the two departing managers described their conversations with the president, the first one said "The president told me to*

leave work immediately and not return." The other person said "The president told me I could stay another couple of weeks."

At the end of the day, as a manager you will be better known (and know better) by what you say you don't know (and ask about), than by what you say you know.

I've encountered many people in business who have poor listening skills. Some of them are in very high positions and appear to be successful. They stand on shaky ground. Their success, both professional and personal, can be shallow and transitory. The people I know who have profound listening skills are nimble and run rings around their less skilled counterparts.

Lesson:

"Shema ul'mad" – Hebrew for "Listen and you will learn."

Chapter Six

Respect

Through the connection of a business acquaintance, I made an appointment to meet with the head of human resources for a major operating unit of a huge corporation. How huge? This company is in the top five of the Fortune 500 in revenue and the top three in profits. My colleague had worked with the company's human resources head, so the arranged meeting acknowledged their professional relationship and mutual respect. The initial e-mails between my colleague and I, and then with the company resulted in a meeting scheduled for one month hence. Less than one week before the scheduled date, the assistant to the head of human resources called me. She was sorry but an urgent company meeting had just been planned and my meeting needed to be pushed back one month. Understanding that emergencies arise, I agreed and set my calendar appropriately.

Two days before the re-scheduled meeting, the assistant called once more. Sorry, but another crisis had arisen and my meeting needed to be re-scheduled again. I offered that I was flexible and would make myself available during off-hours, before or after the workday or during lunchtime, to accommodate the executive's schedule. Thanks, the assistant replied, but we'll need a month to re-schedule the re-scheduling. In a month came a confirming e-mail, re-setting the meeting for three weeks hence.

I won't prolong this story for the length of the four subsequent re-schedulings of re-schedulings of re-schedulings. Three days before the last re-scheduled meeting, the assistant called yet again to say she saw that the executive's calendar was going to be changed, but the assistant would send me an e-mail confirming that she would remind herself to call me in one week to again re-schedule. Forty days after the reminder went unreminded, there was no response from the assistant. I didn't expect a reply and have never received one.

This unprofessional behavior comes from not only a major global company, with a motto that promises "good things," but from one of its human resources executive leaders. Think about it. The human resources head disrespected her assistant who was delegated to do her unpleasant work six times; she disrespected her professional friend, to whom she originally promised a meeting with me; she disrespected her company; and she disrespected herself. Finally, she disrespected her own profession; can you imagine her delivering quality human resources advice and support to her colleagues? I'm more than certain, because I discussed her behavior with people who had similar experiences with her, that this executive didn't feel her behavior or motivations were either unprofessional or rude. What a personal tragedy for her and a daily disaster for the people with and for whom she worked.

Respect isn't about saying "please," "thank you" and "good morning." It is about how you present yourself, how you manage your time, and whether or not you extend your own sense of dignity and self respect to those around you. Respect is shown most effectively in subtle ways. How you listen is a clear demonstration of your respect for others. How you dress is an indicator of your self respect.

Personal authenticity, leadership and respect are mutually supportive and inclusive. The tone and demeanor of your speaking style reflects your respect. The attention you pay to your own actions and the actions of your colleagues signals respect. When your colleagues trust your judgments, always feel you are approachable, and place their faith in your credibility, you have earned their respect. Managers have the added responsibility at work to model respectful and respectable attitudes and behaviors. What managers do and say in the workplace foster the work culture and are seen as the acceptable ways to do business for the organization. *One of the many aspects of Ronald Reagan's approach to the presidency that will be remembered is his stated commitment to hold the office as the employee of the American people, not as their employer. Consider the level of respect inherent in that commitment.*

The Bully Among Us
I once worked with a company president who had risen from being a clerk to managing the largest business in his industry. He knew the

business like few others – every company within the industry either loathed him or wanted to hire him. I once witnessed him ask a person who had done business with him over the phone but had never met him in person, about what that person thought of him. The person, not knowing the subject of her comments was standing in front of her, said, "He's a bastard!" The company president thought that response was hilarious. His reputation was that half the world admired him and the other half hated him, with no one who knew him feeling ambivalent! There was, however, no denying that his was a success story. That is until you got to observe him up close.

For all of his encyclopedic knowledge of the industry (he could shave a dollar a pound off the price in any deal), his financial skills (juggling a profit and loss statement like W.C. Fields with ten cigar boxes), and his track record (the investment analysts salivated as he took his company's stock from pennies to over $40.00 per share), those who knew him well knew he was personally inappropriate, crude, vulgar, profane, and distasteful. What was credited to him rightfully for his material gains in business was more than offset by the debits of his offensive personal characteristics.

But he was successful, right? If the only considerations were the money he accumulated and the material value added to the ledger sheet, yes he was a success. Despite his bravado, he was well aware that he lacked respect, to and from himself. Many who admired him, admired him out of either jealousy or fear. Many who disliked him, disliked him because of either jealousy or personal disgust. Individuals' descriptions of him were constantly followed by the word "but . . ." This was always the conjunction for the clause that excused his disrespectful persona. Who wants to go through life willfully having to be connected to a chain of weak excuses for inexcusable behavior? That is not the definition of success. **"What good will it be for a man if he gains the whole world, yet forfeits his soul?" (Matthew 16:26)**

I conducted a focus group of the company's managers who reported to this president directly. This project was done with the president's knowledge and support. The focus group and I were a thousand miles away from head office. I promised them that everything they wanted to tell me about how they felt managing in the company, I would discuss with the president, with no names attached. I told them he wanted to know, through me, how they felt honestly. Here is what they said,

- "He listens but doesn't hear us."
- "Because of his broken promises, there is a lack of trust."
- "He doesn't have time for me."
- "He won't let me manage."
- "I'm told one thing, then I'm criticized on something else."
- "I'm intimidated."
- "He jumps to conclusions."
- "He doesn't know who I am or what I do, and he doesn't care."
- "The good people in the company don't want to work for him."

When I reported these results to the president, he sat and listened. When I finished, he commented, "All they do is complain." I wondered if he thought I was going to return and give him a list of praises! My response to him was that we needed to address these comments and determine, if they represented the managers' perceptions of him and his style, how we would change that perception. His response was that he didn't want to and wasn't going to change. Within sixteen months, by his own action he was gone from the company.

As in this case, the disrespectful party may well be higher in position (and relative power) in the workplace than the potential targets of the disrespectful behavior. Responding to this behavior poses serious considerations. While it is mandatory that all illegal, discriminatory and harassing actions be reported through the organization's proper channels (often the human resources department) as directed by policy, many times disrespectful behaviors fall short of the legal and policy thresholds of abuse. No one is permitted to abuse you (nor are you permitted to abuse others) and we will discuss this further in a succeeding chapter. *Disrespectful behavior, however, must be addressed just as surely as illegal abuse.*

Left unchecked, disrespectful acts and bullying metastasize into the workplace cancers of harassment, discrimination and retaliation. This lesson was demonstrated in New York City when then Mayor Rudy Giuliani and Police Commissioner Bill Bratton decided to crackdown on what were considered previously to be petty offenses – littering, loitering, public drunkenness and subway fare evasion – using *James Wilson's Broken Windows Theory*. Interestingly, as these petty offenses were tackled effectively, major crimes began to decrease. *Persons who violate the quality of life on the streets (and in the workplace) are the ones who graduate to violating the law (and company policies), if unaddressed.*

How do we respond to disrespectful people and their actions? My colleague Steve counsels and assists executives who have lost their jobs, to enable them to recover and transition to new employment. Steve sees a very broad spectrum of the current business environment. He observes, **"The business climate of civility is worsening. While you may lower your expectations of others, don't let this lower your personal standards."**

The values of respect and self respect being alive and active in the workplace depend upon each of us taking personal responsibility for their maintenance. Similarly, Ann, one of the best executive recruiters I've ever known, states flatly, **"Respect is the bottom-line."**

Paradoxically, researchers in workplace bullying find that the typical reactions of victims of disrespectful behavior can encourage further bullying. Dr. Calvin Morrill of the University of California at Irvine studies corporate culture. He reports, **"What we're finding is that some of the behaviors that we think most protect us are what in fact allow the behavior to continue. Workers become desensitized, tacitly complicit and don't always act rationally."** What that means is that victims often hide from the bully, afraid to confront his or her behavior. Victims may blame other victims or themselves for causing the bullying, rather than addressing the bully's behavior appropriately.

While many organizations have adopted codes of conduct for their employees, others have not progressed to that point of improving the work environment. If your organization has a code, learn it, make sure it is known by your team members and is posted in the workplace. Using an organizational code of conduct to discipline or report disrespectful behavior is the first step you must take when aware of workplace bullying. If a code doesn't exist in your organization, work with human resources to organize and pursue your report effectively.

You should always be forthright in reporting disrespectful behaviors and aware that relatively minor and infrequent disrespects must be handled appropriately differently from major, ongoing bullying. While maintaining your own standards of respectful conduct, you must ensure bullying is either confronted directly by you or reported immediately and accurately; the human resources folks are the right ones to go to first. Keep a record of what you report by composing a concise memo containing the who, what, when, where, why, and witnesses of the events, as discussed previously in Chapter Three. Just your actions of documenting the occurrence and reporting it are generally sufficient to prevent any additional bullying. If, however, additional bullying occurs, your documented record is the basis for stronger correctional measures. *It has been shown time and again that bullies only stop when confronted about their behavior but that when confronted, they back down quickly.*

If your organization doesn't have a code of conduct, lobby your human resources folks to develop one. Many companies have Mission Statements, Vision Statements and/or Social Responsibility Statements. In any of these you will find the core of a code of conduct – you should be familiar with your company's stand on why it exists and you can use these statements to justify the need for a more comprehensive code of conduct. I once wrote a code of conduct for a company in which I had just had to investigate the behavior of its CEO. I had concluded that he hadn't violated any existing company policies or laws, but he had been bullying. Since no statement of expected standards of conduct existed, I proposed one as an integral part of my presentation of findings and recommendations for the board of directors.

I even had the courageous support of the General Counsel. After much debate, the board accepted the findings but rejected the proposed code. In six months, new corporate owners and leadership endorsed and welcomed the code of conduct as the introduction to the employee policy manual. *I kept pushing for what I believed in as right, and with patience the organization was convinced to adopt it.*

Standing in the Middle

Along your journey, you will be involved in plenty of instances in which you are the third party in a dispute, the manager in the middle with the task of bringing two opposing sides together, or at least resolving their conflict. *One of the best methods to bring resolution to antagonistic standoffs is to demonstrate respect for both sides in the dispute.*

Ambassador John Danforth is an Episcopal minister, a former U.S. Senator and a former Special Envoy for the President. During his Senate tenure Danforth, a Republican conservative, was noted for earning the respect and credibility of his colleagues in both parties. When Danforth went to the Sudan to help resolve a crisis involving battling religious factions, he used respect as his first tool in the midst of the conflict. Upon his arrival, he called a meeting between Muslim and Christian leaders. First, the Muslims spoke, declaring everything in their country was fine. Then the Christian leaders set out their "bill of particulars about how they'd been abused." Danforth gave each side the respect of hearing its point of view, without imposing his opinions – and he deftly managed to have the opposing sides listen to each other. Danforth's first impression was "This is really a terrible meeting." That night, however, he hosted both sets of leaders at an embassy reception. And both sets of leaders told him, **"Well, that was a wonderful meeting. You know, we never met each other before."**

Ambassador Danforth's example illustrates a set of simple rules for resolution using the principles of respect when dealing with serious conflicts.

- As the neutral party, you make the opposing parties listen to one another.
- If after listening, each party can re-state and paraphrase what the other side said, it's a good bet they actually heard each other.
- Don't discount conflicting opinions – both parties could be partially correct or they could be saying the same things in

different ways, from different perspectives. *Accepting ambiguity is a key to creative problem solving.*

- In your moderating capacity, after the listening has occurred have each party give you a list of questions for the other side. Exchange the lists and have each party answer the questions, taking alternating turns. This helps each side see issues from the viewpoint of the other side. It is often helpful to ask each party to change places with the other and have a role play. Now they're acting while standing in the other party's shoes. This may lead to developing a compromise solution.
- Come to an agreement on the underlying issues and source of the problem.
- Use your neutral position to show both parties that it takes self respect and strength of character to admit where one is mistaken.
- Have the parties state what they think the other side should do to resolve the conflict. This is where a mutually acceptable compromise will be crafted and implemented.

Customer Service, Customer Sales
Respect translates into productivity and profit. The concept of customer service is at its core the practice of respect in business. Alfredo Molina runs one of America's highest volume jewelry retail stores. He started in the jewelry business when he was eight years old. He tells the following story to prove that everyone "who walks in the door is an important customer" and worthy of respect.

"(A) woman's maid came in to get an opinion on selling a diamond ring to pay for her daughter's education. I spent about 45 minutes with her, explaining the options. In the end, she was so impressed, she told her employer she had to meet Mr. Molina! Over the next five years, that employer spent about $2 million with me – all because of the 45 minutes I spent with her maid."

Looking Inside
Recognizing that true respect begins within, I must admit to my own lapses in paying others and myself the proper respect. One of the fundamental underminers of respect is prejudice. Prejudice is so common in the workplace as an unspoken undercurrent that its negative significance

is often overlooked and missed. For many years I harbored a deep resentment toward the people of Germany because of my unresolved and misdirected feelings of anger about the Holocaust. I tried mightily to suppress this prejudice and convince myself that it didn't affect my interactions with colleagues.

Then the company for which I worked was bought by a German concern that was an arm of the German government. It is said that God moves in mysterious ways! Feelings I had tried to cover up came bubbling to the surface. I struggled in my heart to push those feelings back down and cover them. I don't believe I ever expressed my prejudiced feelings in the workplace or ever let them influence the performance of my duties, but those weren't the real problems. I didn't change my motivations for this behavior.

Shortly after the merger and acquisition of my employer, I met Robert. He was the newly appointed head of global security and one of his first tasks was to organize the security function in the U.S. Before he could address that issue, he was presented with a massive security breakdown in one of the largest U.S. offices. Robert called me. We had never met and on his trip to the U.S. he wanted to get together with me. While Robert's English was fluent, his German accent was pure and strong. I admit to cringing when I first heard his voice.

Robert enlisted my help with his mission from the beginning. "Tony," he said, "you are human resources and we need to work together. (The acquiring company's CEO) told me you are the guy to see and trust, so let's meet in Miami." Robert had no idea what I looked like, what kind of a colleague I was, or from where I came. It didn't matter to him.

He put his trust in me and showed his respect and authenticity by acknowledging and asking for my cooperation. I went to Miami with two of my human resource colleagues and two members of the U.S. security team to meet and work with him.

My first impression of Robert was of his warm smile. He was relaxed, cheerful and welcoming. He took my hand, grinned and said, "Thanks for coming to help me." This was an authentic person with a healthy, balanced ego and an open personality. Robert wasn't the German I envisioned, expected or thought I disliked. When we all met in his hotel room for the first time, he asked each of us what we wanted to drink, he invited us to sit in a semi-circle, and he listened thoughtfully and respectfully to all of our opinions and observations. It was only after each of us had a chance to speak that Robert suggested how we could work as a team to solve the problems at hand. He deferred to our suggestions, commenting that we understood the U.S. operations and culture far better than he did. He directed that each two-person investigative team have one security member and the other member be from human resources. "We must make sure," he instructed, "that everyone we talk to be protected and given his full rights and respect." I had seldom seen law enforcement investigations in which I took part conducted with more adherence to protecting the dignity of the involved parties.

During our time together in Miami, an important soccer match was taking place in Europe. Robert told us he was a dedicated soccer fan – he actually described himself as "nuts" about the sport and especially about the German national team. This particular match was being broadcast everywhere it seemed except to Miami. Those of us working with Robert in Miami could tell he regretted not being able to follow the match live. We devised a plan – call Robert's assistant in Germany, have the assistant turn on the radio broadcast there, and have Robert listen to it on speakerphone in the Miami office! It seemed clever enough. The workday dragged on into the evening, well after the match had begun. With our last interview over, we found an empty office and sprung the plan on Robert. His face lit up like a kid's at a birthday party as he sat and listened to the final period. I sat with him and at every crucial save and scoring opportunity happening thousands of miles away, Robert would pump his fist and cheer. There was no self-conscious reticence or pretense about him; he was comfortable being himself in the company of others. I was very impressed by him and equally ashamed of myself.

In the aftermath of the events of September 11, 2001, Robert sent a message to his colleagues in the U.S. In it he said that as a former member of the German army and as a human being he was shocked by the cowardly and dastardly nature of the attack, sympathetic with his American friends, and proud of the stance of the world in support of this country. With a few simple words he showed the depth of his profound respect for his colleagues. In contrast, the CFO and temporary head of global human resources for the parent company was an ex-pat American stationed in Europe. He remained silent and sent no message of support to his fellow countrymen.

I eventually told Robert that by being the person he was and through my friendship with him, I learned how ignorant and self-destructive my own prejudice about Germans had been. His example of respect forced me to re-examine my weak profession of respect. It wasn't sufficient for me to lecture my colleagues about a respectful workplace when I wasn't paying attention to my own feelings. *The first place to look for and eradicate prejudice in the workplace was in my own heart. Genuine respect starts there, as well.*

Being Baited
You can be attacked with disrespect so suddenly that you are caught off-guard. With the head of human resources for an organization I served as Chief Administrative Officer, I took a trip to a research facility in the Midwest to finalize the integration of one of its units that my organization had acquired. As a portent of things to come, our flight out of New York was delayed and then cancelled. We waited at the airport for seven hours until a new flight was scheduled. Despite the first-class seats we were given in consolation, the flight was uncomfortable. By the time we landed I was in great physical pain from too much sitting and far too much tension. As I drove the rental to the university, all I could think about were the dozens of action items still unfinished for the integration. Apparently, I was thinking about them exclusively because a state trooper pulled me over for driving 40mph in a 20 mph zone. I hadn't noticed the speed limit change from the highway to the local road! My first and only speeding ticket. Imagine my mood arriving at the offices of the unit being acquired: in pain, cranky about the ticket, had a headache, was hungry, thirsty and worried about uncompleted business.

The founder of the unit, a grim-faced researcher, met me and saw I wasn't doing well. He sent out for some pain reliever and invited my human resources colleague and me into his office. There he began a three-minute shouting and cursing tirade about the lack of a completed benefits package for his staff. I timed it – three minutes. I said nothing. I watched calmly as his temper and his manners spun out of control. The redder in the face he got, the calmer I became. I remembered an East African friend telling me a saying from his country, **"When two elephants fight, it is the ground that suffers."** I wasn't going to fight with him, although I was in no mood for this disrespectful outburst. I also knew it was calculated to catch me off-guard so that I would either lose my temper in response (and ignore my own values) or cave-in and agree to a different benefits plan being pushed by the founder that wasn't the best business deal.

When the founder was finished, I observed that he was out of steam and almost foaming at the mouth. I hadn't taken up the challenge, so he had worked himself into a frenzy without the desired result. I stood up, looked at my human resources colleague, then at the founder and said, "You need to calm down. And you need to show my office and my team the proper respect. If there is a real issue here, we'll fix it before we leave." I turned to the door and informed my colleague that we were going to now visit with each member of the unit's staff and take note of all concerns and open issues. We left the doctor panting and sweating in his office.

Outside of the office, my colleague complained, "I'm so angry with him. He was rude and he disrespected you." I replied, "Yes he did and he was, but he didn't get what he wanted. I didn't disrespect him or myself."

I also knew that the founder realized he made a mistake. Lacking the screaming match he thought he could provoke, he had not gained any ground. Subsequent investigation showed that there were personal reasons why he wanted the benefits plan he was trying to promote over the one eventually chosen. After I completed my individual visits with the staff, the doctor approached me and took me aside. "I'm sorry for blowing up like that," he told me. "I know you and your folks will do the right thing for this operation." Without my firing a shot in defense, I defeated his offensive behavior. *Often the most respectful and productive response to someone throwing fire at you is to return with a dousing of water.*

Your Assignments

You are responsible for taking the following best practice steps to establish and maintain a respectful workplace –

- *Be aware*. Be sure of where you stand on respect in the workplace and where your organization stands. Ensure your team members are aware of and have access to copies of the code of conduct, anti-harassment, and anti-discrimination policies that are posted conspicuously in the workplace. Take time every year to hold a discussion on these codes and policies with your team. Be ready to hear complaints and suggestions and to act upon this information at any time.
- *Model appropriate respectful behavior in the workplace.* You are the leader – what you do and tolerate others will emulate. If you have to discipline someone, do it behind closed doors, face to face and with a managerial or human resources witness present. Similarly, if you offend someone in public, then apologize in public as well. Make yourself available to listen to your colleagues, customers and peers.
- *Treat yourself with respect.* If you have no respect for yourself, no one will have any for you. Be mindful of how and what you say, your personal appearance, and what you allow to be said or done to you. If you look and treat yourself like a doormat, you will be used like one by others.
- *Scour your heart of prejudice.* It's wrong, you know it's wrong, and no matter how you think you may be guarding it, it will pop out to your eternal detriment.
- *Be mindful and respectful of the time of others.* Return e-mails, letters, memos and voicemails within 24 hours of receipt, even if only to acknowledge your awareness and say you'll get back in more detail later. Keep to your schedule and notify others if

you will be late. Re-schedule meetings ONLY due to unforeseen emergencies: the people with whom you have an established meeting take precedence over others for that time period. Never re-schedule more than once.

- *Ensure meetings aren't disrupted by ringing phones, beeping pagers, buzzing cellphones and personal interruptions.* If the incoming information must be addressed, apologize to the meeting participants, call a break and set a time to resume as quickly that day as possible.
- *Establish clear standards* for the appropriate ways visitors and colleagues are greeted and attended to, how telephones are answered, and how e-mails and correspondence are composed.
- *Never transfer a visitor or a caller to someone else in the organization without first finding out what the outside person wants*, determining who can be of assistance, and letting the outsider know you can be called back if needed.
- *Be responsible for your work environment.* If there is a piece of paper in the hallway, pick it up. Have inappropriate, offensive and unprofessional materials, such as unrelated magazines, cartoons and posters, removed from the workplace.
- *Counsel colleagues* who yell on telephone calls and use inappropriate language and gestures in the workplace to stop or be disciplined.
- *Do unto others as you would have them do unto you.* **Matthew 7:12**

Lesson:

"If we are to prevail as a free, self-governing people, we must first govern our tongues and our pens. Restoring civility to public discourse is not an option. It is a necessity." Ed Feulner, President of the Heritage Foundation

Chapter Seven

Out in the open

I think all of us, including me carry thoughts and deeds that to some degree we don't necessarily want to reveal to others. Nevertheless, there are times when these circumstances find their way out in the open, in the workplace.

I've faced my share of issues out in the open at work. There have been times when I've made a thought-out, conscious decision that the issue could not be brought to light completely, without major negative consequences. For example, I've dealt with a number of colleagues who were quite clearly alcoholics – I smelled it, I observed it, I sensed it strongly. So long as their work and the work environment were not affected by it, there were both legal and privacy considerations that constrained me from raising the issue directly. (There are 28 states plus Washington, D. C. where local laws prohibit employers from "discriminating against employees" due to workers' off-duty participation in lawful activities such as smoking and drinking alcohol.) Many alcoholics I've met in the workplace were very functional, many of them at a fairly sophisticated level. They do not stumble or slur their words or pass out at their desks, in the stereotypical behaviors we've come to expect from alcohol dependent people. In fact, they've perfected their defense mechanisms and compensating skills to cleverly avoid outright detection. This makes the manager's confrontation of this issue extremely difficult.

Sometimes I've tried to work around it – in one instance, I solicited a mutual friend, not employed by my organization, to ask my colleague gingerly if he was having a drinking problem. Even that bit of detached subterfuge was approached with a lot of trepidation. I've re-distributed employee assistance program materials, making sure they are left on every desk, including the colleague in need. I've held impromptu meetings to remind all colleagues about the organization's substance abuse policy and the availability of confidential counseling through the benefits program. I've tried to be creative. I've prayed.

My focus in these circumstances is always on work performance issues, not my attempts to regulate personal behaviors, despite the practical consequence that it is the personal behaviors that need to change. When the "morning after syndrome" effects the workplace, warnings and disciplinary actions may be warranted. But that colleague is still a fellow human being, in need of motivation to change his or her behavior. *Out in the open problems present their own set of management challenges.*

Your journey as a manager will be marked with times when you will have to make similar judgments, encounter the same delicate problems, and choose what and how much comes out in the open. Using the tools we've discussed so far, your ability and skills to manage in these situations will be strengthened considerably in comparison to times previously. It is clear that these demanding situations require empathic listening and a keen awareness of your own motives and the motives of others involved.

Managing In the Light

These situations are shrouded in ambiguity, testing your leadership skills. When you are dealing with sensitive issues among your colleagues, your personal authenticity and the organization's commitment to treating employees with respect and dignity are tested.

- *Managing issues out in the open that effect the workplace, including issues that touch you personally, can only be done successfully if you manage the other, upfront issues with honesty, logical compassion, openness and a solid leadership presence.* When you can manage the improbable on a daily basis, managing the seemingly impossible is doable; it just takes a bit longer!
- *Faced with the potentially explosive out in the open situation, turn to others for information and support while maintaining your position of leadership in the matter.* You will find that every time you share an insurmountable problem with a trusted colleague, your manager or a human resources professional, the

climb up and over that mountain becomes easier. Even leaders don't have to go it alone.

- *Using discretion, always check with colleagues inside your organization and peers in other companies (remember consultants with whom you've developed working friendships) to see what was done in similar situations.* There are no current situations at work that don't share similar characteristics with past situations, that were eventually either resolved or from which lessons were learned. In this regard, human resources colleagues are excellent, sometimes off the record, sources of assistance.
- *Keep in mind that most big problems are compilations of smaller issues and circumstances* – unvoiced work frustrations, spikes in workload volumes, unfounded rumors. Before trying to conquer the big out in the open problem, break it down into smaller, more manageable problems and enlist support in resolving those first. The big problem often fades away once you start addressing its component parts.
- *Just listen.* As we talked about before, what may appear to be an unexpected crisis may in truth be your colleagues needing someone to hear them.
- *Don't allow other agendas to replace your management responsibilities*. As an authentic leader, you adapt your problem solving approach to fit the practical work necessities without letting yourself be pulled away from your goal to lead your team to success consistent with your values. The ways you manage problems must be flexible, your motivation as a manager and your faith must be firm.
- *Reject the false and seductive notion of situational ethics.* The concept and practice of ethics don't require a modifier. Tainted means result in tainted ends and they don't justify each other. There is right and there is wrong.
- *Make time your ally* – problems have a way of untangling and revealing themselves given appropriate time and space. I'm not saying don't act; I'm saying act judiciously without rushing yourself blindly. This goes back to managing ambiguity – the more you learn about a problem, the clearer it becomes. Inaction

is not a substitute for successful action BUT hasty reaction is a sure path to failure. I was once instructed, "Sometimes no decision is a decision."

- ***Honor your own inner reflection and insight.*** Your inner light is there for a purpose. That problem that just jumped out into the open only appears to be baffling. When you feed your inner resources with valid information and perform enough contemplation and prayer to let that information sink in, you will be surprised at just how well equipped you are to manage that problem down to size and whip it.

The "It" Surprise
Along your journey, you will also meet people, some of whom will be your peers or outrank you organizationally, who unleash personality traits out into the open, traits that will be embarrassing at best and harmful at worst. How do you manage in these situations? Donald Trump (of all managers!) offers a word of caution about employees whose negative behaviors come out in the open unexpectedly.

"You can interview somebody for an hour or two hours, and never know what you're hiring until you get them in the job. To a certain extent, it's chance. There are many people that give great interviews and are lousy employees, and then there are people who give terrible job interviews and are fabulous employees . . . You go with that person who maybe has that extra 'it' quality, and the 'it' quality turns out to be not so good."

This is a good reminder that as a manager, you must be aware of what is going on around you at all times, to proactively detect that negative 'it' and deal with 'it' before 'it' comes out in the open and becomes a full blown disaster. I have been fooled in interviews I've conducted. There is no other word for it – I allowed myself to be fooled because when the 'it' came out, 'it' was so glaring I kicked myself in the pants for not seeing 'it' before I made the hire.

I hired a human resources manager at one time, to be posted to a large and sensitive company installation. This place had unions, organized crime influences, a history of sexual harassment claims, adulterous relationships among employees and managers, bribery plots, extortion and murders – it was a serious place with serious problems! Before I hired this person, I went to lunch with him and the recruiter on my team. The opinions were all favorable – the manager of the installation liked him and the recruiter recommended him. As a candidate for the job, he was enthusiastic and full of energy and ideas, just what was required at this installation. Instead of sitting down with him in my office and having an in-depth discussion about his conception of the job and knowledge of human resources best practices, I punted at lunch and said, "Everyone gives you a thumbs up so you're hired." I didn't look into him until after he came onboard.

I was soon regretting my hasty judgment. Although he constantly reminded me that he had over 20 years of human resources experience, those 20 years couldn't have been recent. He commented on the age of an employee in a company e-mail discussing that employee's ability to perform a certain job. He was about to hand a terminated employee a severance agreement, without giving him the legally required waiting period to discuss the document with his attorney.

The final straw and the most glaring out in the open behavior came when I received a complaint letter from a job applicant, sent via the human resources global office in Switzerland. You just know this applicant had to be pretty steamed to send his complaint all the way to Europe! The applicant claimed he had been treated less than professionally by the human resources manager in an interview. Among other things, the applicant stated he was given only seven minutes for the interview from start to finish, after being made to wait past the scheduled appointment time. The human resources manager said it wasn't true. A review of the visitor log substantiated the complaint. I directed the manager to send a letter of apology. I had counseled him after each incident but after the third, the thin ice he was on was about to break.

I was 100% responsible for hiring the wrong person for the job. He was not a "bad" person, just not the person for this job. Unfortunately for him, his job performance made his new position expendable in the next round of budget cuts. My error had not only cost him a job, it had cost the company a vital position. I was heartsick that he lost his job, I am every time someone loses a job in my organization, but I was angrier at myself for not probing his character for what should have been obvious to me. He gave a great interview and a sub par performance. His "show" was a mile wide but his "substance" was a millimeter thick, thus demonstrating Mr. Trump's wisdom.

Dependencies

Want some sobering news about out in the open behavior at work? A report by the respected substance abuse testing laboratory Quest Diagnostics states that while the abuse of drugs such as cocaine, marijuana, opiates and acid at work have either declined or remained flat, the use of amphetamines (in both the legal and illegal versions) at work has increased "in epidemic proportions." This translates into an alarming 44% jump in use at work from 2003 to 2004. The Quest director of science and technology Dr. Barry Sample warns, "Employees on amphetamines may be doing their work faster, but they're probably doing it wrong – faster."

Aside from drug abuse at work, I've found alcohol abuse to be the leading substance abuse factor hidden by a significant proportion of colleagues with whom I've worked. According to the World Health Organization, alcohol use accounts for 4% of all deaths worldwide and is the #1 risk factor for deaths among males ages 15 to 59.

As I stated at the beginning of this chapter, I've had co-workers who literally reeked of alcohol – I knew one soul with a heart of pure gold, whose small office smelled of whiskey even when he wasn't occupying it. He drank before work, probably at lunchtime, and for sure after work. There was never a time when I could say he was drunk at work. Neither I nor anyone else ever caught him drinking on company time. In the state in which we worked, an employee could not be disciplined for suspected substance abuse unless his or her condition at work was reviewed by an individual specifically trained and qualified to determine substance abuse.

I took that training; however, I realized it was an uphill struggle to address the abuse issue without risking delving into areas of individual privacy. My colleague was functional – as have been the vast majority of alcoholic co-workers I've suspected and known. I attempted all the covert strategies I outlined previously involving employee assistance programs and policy reminders. In the case of this particular colleague, I stayed on guard about his behaviors at work, paid special attention to any signs of incidents with his colleagues and prayed he would find his way to self-awareness. *I'm still praying.* He performed his work, but he continued to destroy himself physically.

A senior executive vice president with whom I had the privilege to work for some time once confided in me that his son had a dreadful substance abuse problem. This executive was also a devout Catholic who practiced logical compassion. Shaking his head in frustration at the years his son lost in the battle for sobriety, the executive gave me the best advice I'd ever heard about dealing within one's self about a friend, relative or colleague with this problem. He said, **"In the end, you just have to love them. Not coddle them or facilitate their dependency, but just love them."**

There are problems that come out like phantoms, floating around the workplace and touching down but never settling. As managers we find ourselves managing through these problems, never quite able to grab on and wrestle them to the ground. *We must recognize and accept this; these troubled colleagues are still human beings.* They may need counseling, discipline about work performance, or to be separated from the organization but they never cease to be individual people with all too human problems.

Opening Strategies
But we are not without managerial strategies and best practices for dealing with suspected alcohol and substance abuse in the workplace, successfully.

- Have a clearly worded, strong policy that prohibits the use of alcohol, all non-medically prescribed drugs, all controlled substances (pot, cocaine, etc.), and the misuse of prescribed drugs in the workplace, during the workday, while using work vehicles and equipment, and while conducting the organization's business. Publish this policy, distribute it to everyone, and post it conspicuously. Ensure all employees sign for their receipt of the distributed copies.

- Ensure you and your managers and supervisors review and discuss this policy at least annually with all employees. Everyone in your work group must know where you and the organization stand on this issue.

- Make sure your organization is enrolled in an Employee Assistance Program (EAP) and use it. EAPs are low- or no-cost benefits, usually attached to the organization's healthcare or life insurance coverage. They provide advice and counseling to employees on a confidential basis and promote proactive healthcare strategies through newsletters, programs and discounts (nutritional information, exercise regimens and health club membership assistance). One of the significant features offered by EAPs is guidance for organizations for managing alcohol and substance abuse issues. EAPs provide awareness training for managers, educational materials for employees and referrals for professional counseling.

- Train yourself and your supervisors to recognize the signs of alcohol and substance abuse, the laws that apply in the workplace, and the resources available (Employee Assistance Programs and treatment options sponsored by healthcare insurance providers). EAPs almost always give this training for free to their subscribers.

- Understand the application of any local laws and of the Americans With Disabilities Act (ADA) in cases of suspected or confirmed alcohol and substance abuse in the workplace. The ADA does not protect employees under the influence of alcohol or illegal substances from being disciplined for performance problems. It does protect employees who are former alcohol or substance abusers, who have sought or are seeking substance abuse treatment, or who are incorrectly determined by the organization to be substance abusers, from being discriminated against at work because of the substance abuse. This is the complicated aspect of applying the protections of the ADA. If you or your organization are already aware an employee has a substance abuse problem and/or sought treatment for this problem previously, it is likely the ADA's protections will require your organization to reasonably accommodate re-newed or continued treatment. That means not firing the employee, allowing him or her reasonable time off to attend treatment (including the possibility of a flexible work schedule), and not taking any adverse employment action (demotion, substantial negative change in work circumstances, etc.) against the employee due to the substance abuse. The organization can require the employee to guarantee in writing that he or she will attend the treatment, with attendance reports given to the organization, as a condition for receiving this reasonable accommodation.

- Remember, the ADA's limitation for what is reasonable for an organization to accommodate is that by doing so, an organization does not impose an "undue" hardship on itself. For example, an organization does not have to create a "light duty" job as an accommodation where such a job has never existed before and does not fit the business' needs. An accommodated employee's behavior at work is still subject to the same policies, rules and management that apply to all other colleagues. An employee cannot commit an act of workplace harassment or a crime, and not expect to be disciplined or discharged as appropriate to the actual circumstances. It is important for managers to understand and practice fair and appropriate discipline that is not retaliatory for all employees regardless of any ADA claims.

- Be aware that an employee with an alcohol or substance abuse problem, who is encouraged and helped to recover and return to work, will nearly always become a loyal and grateful employee. Yes, some people do fall off the wagon and some never attain the self-realization that it's time to recover. These people are in a small minority. Help people to change their motivation and you help them change their behavior. Logical compassion requires managers to see the human side of a problem situation, act authentically, apply policy and law fairly and evenly, and take the reasonable steps to bring a colleague who wants and needs help back into the workplace as a productive teammate.

- Investigate and act on any complaints of substance abuse, possession or distribution in the workplace. Involve your organization's legal counsel, human resources professionals and security. The organization may need to bring in an outside security provider or law enforcement to assist in determining if illegal activities are occurring within its areas of responsibility.

When dealing with accidents on the job that are suspected of being caused by alcohol or drug use, your first course of action is to determine if anyone is injured, and if so to provide immediate medical assistance. You will need to act swiftly – while assessing and assisting in the situation, you will be presented with lots of fragments of information, much of it seemingly ambiguous. Where was the injured person working? What was he or she doing? Who saw this? What did you see? But your primary goal is first-aid help. It's always the best practice to have a number of employees certified in CPR and a sufficient first-aid kit on hand.

Secondly, know when to alert medical professionals and have injured persons assisted to the hospital. In the case of suspected alcohol or substance abuse, immediate medical care is the number one consideration: your organization's policies must state that you have the right to require professional substance abuse testing in all accident situations. Your suspicions have to be reasonable (staggered walking, slurred speech, strong odor of alcohol, violent and wild mannerisms and actions, sleeping on the job) and you should always have human resources accompany you in making this determination. If an employee involved in a workplace accident tests positive for substance abuse or refuses to take such a test mandated by policy, the incident must be documented thoroughly and the subject employee disciplined or discharged. Have your organization's legal counsel and human resources professional included in making the appropriate determination.

Pre-Employment Tools
The federal Department of Transportation requires commercial truck drivers to take part in mandatory substance abuse testing on a regular basis. Generally speaking, states and some localities do not permit

random substance abuse testing of current employees, unless they are involved in safety-critical work (nuclear power plant operators) and the random testing includes everyone (senior management, too). It is legal to require substance testing prior to hiring prospective employees, so long as they consent to it beforehand in writing and it is conducted according to federal and local mandates. In these instances, employment is expressly reserved for those prospects who pass the substance tests (test "negative" for the presence of illegal substances).

Depending on what your organization is prepared to invest in such tests, a technologically advanced test of a human hair sample can accurately determine substance use going back several years. I have heard some intriguing explanations from prospective employees as to why they tested "positive" for substance use, including;

- "I was in a room where everyone but me was smoking dope and I inhaled."
- "I'm on an experimental medicine that mimics cocaine use in drug tests."
- "I just smoked one reefer to party the night before I took the drug test."

It is important for you and your organization to keep in mind that as long as these are prospective hires and your application of the testing policy is consistent, there is no obligation to re-test or re-consider persons who test "positive," for employment. Use an established, respected testing company and rely on them to address any questionable situations and issues concerning pre-employment substance testing, with prospective employees. This testing is one reliable way you can bring hidden behaviors out before you make a hiring decision.

Another tool is pre-employment, post-offer background checks. The administration of these comes under the legal regulation of the Fair Credit Reporting Act (FCRA). Many employers have education, employment, convictions and driving records checked. Some also include credit history (especially in the banking, securities and accounting sectors). Prospective hires must be provided with a written statement of their

FCRA rights and give their signed permission prior to the check being done. Every organization for which I have worked has contracted out background checking to one of the many firms that provide this service. The checking is done swiftly (usually within 10 to 15 days depending on the elements being checked and the jurisdictions covered) and the results reported back to the hiring entity confidentially.

The organization must be careful to keep its receipt and review of these results strictly confidential. State law in California requires prospective employers to provide a copy of the results to prospective employees. The Fair and Accurate Credit Transactions Act (FACT) amends FCRA concerning investigations done for an organization by a third-party (a vendor) concerning an employee. Pre-employment investigations are not covered by the FACT provisions.

It is a best practice to have one senior human resources professional receive and analyze the results and communicate with the hiring manager. This communication should be limited to whether or not the prospective hire "passed" the background check. Because the organization's employment application contains (or should contain) a statement that giving false information will disqualify an applicant from consideration for employment (and the applicant signed the statement), any substantial discrepancy between the applicant provided information and the background results is reasonable cause to not hire.

- o Criminal checks should consider only misdemeanors and felonies, not traffic tickets or desk appearances tickets (called Adjournments in Contemplation of Dismissal or ACDs in some places).
- o Criminal checks should extend backward for a reasonable time period, usually 5 to 7 years, although some jobs (security guard, chemist in a pharmaceuticals lab) would reasonably extend back further.
- o College degrees and work experience are by far the two top categories for finding discrepant information.

Just as with pre-employment substance testing, pre-employment background checks are "PRE" not "POST." Don't begin the final official, legal employment relationship before you've obtained all of the available information to make a considered conclusion. Employment offers must be conditional. If you bring someone onboard before the test and background results are in, and then discover that out in the open pops a convicted embezzler who is now your senior accounts payable manager, you're going to have to fire a current onboard employee, instead of withdrawing a conditional offer. We'll discuss the common law doctrines that apply in these instances, in the later chapter on the law and the Appendix.

But you know, the employment situation isn't always so simple – the general rule is that persons convicted (not arrested, arrest records can't be considered and shouldn't be available) of a crime cannot be disqualified for employment unless their specific convicted offense is directly related to the specific responsibilities of the proposed job. A person convicted of drunk driving shouldn't be considered for a truck driver or forklift operator but should be considered, if qualified, for a file clerk. Most localities want to encourage the employment of released offenders. This advice pre-supposes that your employment application asks the direct question, "Have you been convicted of a misdemeanor or felony in the last seven years and if so, please give details," and that the applicant answered the question truthfully. Because if the applicant lied, then the decision to no longer consider him or her for employment is automatic.

Legal Tools
Let's discuss behavior that is conducted not so openly in the workplace. You are told by an employee that a colleague is storing a gun in his or her locker at work. Your organization's policy prohibits the possession of a weapon at work, except by security personnel. You ask around and determine that the colleague in question has shown the gun in his locker to other co-workers. You approach both human resources and corporate security with this information. The locker is clearly company property. As a group, you meet with your general counsel and present what you've heard and suspect. What is the next step? Your counsel may cite the U.S. Supreme Court case of O'Connor v. Ortega (1987). The justices decided that the purpose for a workplace search must be based on either real business needs (looking for a file and coming upon

something else) or a reasonable suspicion. The search must be "justified at its inception" and "justified in scope." That scope must be limited to achieve what is needed for that purpose. Led by security, you search the locker and find a weapon, in violation of policy. You take appropriate action based upon that finding – you don't then search the employee's car.

In the same vein, the absolute necessity for e-mail in conducting business raises issues related to searching and monitoring the e-mail system. The Electronics Communications Privacy Act allows organizations to search their e-mail system, where the system is utilized by the entire organization and there is no reasonable expectation of privacy. Your organization's policies should include a statement that the e-mail system is for business purposes only and will be monitored routinely as part of the ordinary course of business. The flipside to this issue is the mandate of the Telecommunications Act of 1996 that imposes criminal liability for persons (including your employees) sending or allowing to be sent "indecent materials" online or via networks to which minors have access. Like obscene materials e-mailed from work to people's homes or vice-versa.

You may be asking, so what about telephone calls at work, can't the organization monitor those? For quality control purposes yes, so long as you announce upfront "This call may be recorded and monitored for quality control purposes." Wiretapping is another matter. The Federal Wiretapping Act (also known as the Omnibus Crime Control and Safe Streets Act of 1968) does allow surreptitious monitoring of telephone calls if it is in the "ordinary course of business." Each instance must be evaluated separately on its own merits and justified. There must be reasonable suspicion, it must be done during office hours, and the conversations must be between employees. If it ever gets to the point where you or your organization are seriously considering wiretapping employee telephone conversations, take a deep breath, exhale slowly and have a long talk with your general counsel, human resources and the other managers involved. Wiretapping at work isn't worth the potential embarrassment and damage to credibility. Wiretapping employees isn't something you want to come out in the open.

Media: Social or Business

The upsurge in use of social media (texting, Facebook, blogging, etc.) by employees in and about the workplace presents new challenges out in the open, the effects of which are being explored legally. While employees may not transmit, without specific permission, confidential information using these media, critical comments about work and employers may well be permissible by law, especially if these communications are between employees genuinely concerned about work issues. Moreover, the law permits a certain amount of profanity by workers in these communications, when they are legitimately talking about work issues.

Is Your HR Department a Too Silent Partner?

Strangely enough, some of the most frequent organizational complaints about managers who hide are directed at human resources. Why do employees only see human resources when they're hired and if they have a benefits or payroll problem? I think you can tell by now that I am fairly demanding of myself and the other members of my profession. Human resources exists to serve your needs and further the organization's goals in the workplace. To do that human resources can neither consider nor act as if its main job is to process transactions (hiring paperwork, insurance enrollments, employee separation forms). The human resources unit that focuses on the transactional aspects of its responsibilities isn't human resources, it is bookkeeping.

For us to serve you, we must be strategic – planning, recruiting and supporting hirings that last; monitoring, developing and improving cost-effective benefits programs that meet employees' real and changing needs; creating, implementing and leading cutting edge training and development; identifying and fostering potential talents outside of and within the organization; educating and advising managers – all to enhance the quality of the work environment, culture and experience. Disappointingly, an unhealthy proportion of human resource departments are managed with the aim of filling and filing the paperwork, focused on the end products of transactional service, not the qualitative strategic inputs that must dictate that service.

I once asked a group of learned managers in an educational not-for-profit how human resources had failed them. To a professional person, each one lit up with interest and described a reactive, process driven human resources function that was unseen until someone needed to change his or her insurance coverage! What did they say they wanted from human resources?

- **"A business partner who is in front of, not lagging behind, change."**
- **"Proactive professionals, with the knowledge and credibility to give upfront advice."**
- **"Pros in the meetings with us, helping us build our plans."**

A human resources team that is seen, heard, felt, listened to, listening, respected and followed. If we in human resources don't deliver that level of strategic service to you, we deserve to be replaced with interactive computer screens, so that you can do the transactional work yourselves, quicker and cheaper! Why pay for a business function that adds no value? Human resources hidden away adds no value and it's hardly "human." *And it is not honoring its own "soul at work."*

I've met and known a lot of human resources professionals. I can divide them into four categories: the Directory Crew who are stuck in the era of the Personnel Department and can't do much more than sign up employees and file forms; the Rote Squad who fell into human resources because there wasn't anywhere else to go in the corporate world where they could collect a paycheck; the Burnouts who have been stressed to the max and take it out on those they serve; and the Strategic Team who are customer service oriented, proactive business partners with the rest of management. By far the smallest group is the latter – I know the human resources folks reading this aren't pleased to hear that but I stand by it. We members of this profession don't come out in the open and tackle the complex problems of the modern workplace often and effectively enough.

We in human resources work for you. *Human resources exists to support you as the managerial backbone of the organization.* It is basically impossible for you to perform at your peak effectiveness if we aren't right with you providing assistance, guidance, training, encouragement, moral ammunition, practical solutions, expertise, and innovation. We must keep you and ourselves *out* in the open and *in* the daily, minute-by-minute life of the workplace for management to be successful.

Let me tell you about one human resources executive I knew. I experienced him at work. He was my peer. The disaster he wrought survives his retirement to this very day. He was so **not** in the open, he was out – managing to be nowhere when he was everywhere. Everywhere except where he should have been.

He believed that his only customer was the CEO, and his only viewpoint was the CEO's viewpoint. His only tactics were the CEO's tactics. The CEO was his only reference. He therefore narrowed his field of vision and range of motion to a space roughly equivalent to the short walk between his office and the CEO's. Whenever I spoke with him, every other sentence began with words like "Edward thinks . . ." and "Edward believes . . . ," invoking the CEO's first name. He was so stuck inside his CEO's personality that he couldn't see how sightless he himself really was. But everyone with whom he came in contact saw his disability immediately.

His staff made it no secret to my human resources team and me that the first order of business each day was to gauge their boss' mood and restrict their interface with him accordingly. If an opinion didn't match his CEO's, it triggered one of his well known outbursts. I suspected that hidden inside of him was his authentic self, probably unused and left alone for a couple of decades, stretching back to when he started in human resources and worked in support of, not apart from his colleagues.

One of the paradoxes in this story is that the CEO he followed slavishly ran a company that spilled red ink like a pump. Tens of millions of dollars a year. Unhappy, unproductive workers and angry, dissatisfied stockholders. Each year, the parent company bought the CEO's story that another $25 million down the drain and we'll turn this baby around. How authentically was the parent company being managed?

This human resources executive came to deliver some bad news to a group of colleagues with whom I worked. His visit came after a year of my arguing and pleading that he needed to show his face to this group, even if he didn't have all the answers to their questions or he didn't know what was going to happen to them or he was only meeting with them to become acquainted. For over a year he rejected my reasoning that his presence was as important as the decision he would ultimately deliver. He was simply too busy zigzagging across the country, dragging his boss' messages to the troops like a hound dog with a tattered bone. I talked with many colleagues in his company. They were unanimous in their opinion of the quality of their work lives – it was the pits. Human resources was a massive force of ever changing faces that managed to keep itself important to the corporate brass but a nonfactor in improving the work environment for managers and the rank and file.

Just how abysmal his human resources service delivery was, and how not in the open, became abundantly obvious when I met one of the computer operations senior managers in his company. This manager attended a conference with managers from my company. During the conference, an administrative assistant entered the room to deliver some supplies. The computer operations senior manager took one look at her and announced, "Come over here honey and stand by me. You can pour my coffee all day long." Of course this was reported back to me and I registered a formal complaint with the human resources executive. He responded that his computer colleague was "a little backward" but, not to worry, he would be spoken to about the comment. I barely restrained my anger and replied that after he was "spoken to" perhaps he could be referred back to me so that I could read the anti-harassment and code of conduct policies to him. No, I was told, that wouldn't be necessary because, after all, my company's policies didn't cover that manager's employment! Yes, by the way, I did speak with the offending manager and informed him that while in my company's offices, his behavior was governed by my company's policies. He wasn't very appreciative of my instruction but he did listen. *Like it or not, he was required to respect his colleagues.*

The time came for the human resources executive to talk to my colleagues about their futures (or lack of same) with the consolidation of our two companies. The only two memorable parts of his presentation to the group were:

1. He commented out loud about the quality of his silk shirt, and
2. His presentation was filled with references, quotes and pictures of his CEO.

Without exception, each of my colleagues present at his talk came back to me later and said they would have preferred to receive the bad news of their displacement from me. One colleague, referring to the executive, commented, "He should have continued to stay home and press his silk shirt!" I listened to their complaints and helped them with their concerns. Although the executive had left a mess in the aftermath of his presentation, I set about with my team to clean it up and provide the services my colleagues needed.

As my team and I cooperated with the executive's human resources team, who outnumbered us ten to one but underperformed us by the same ratio, it was no shock that no one in his shop could make an independent decision. The executive made all the decisions but he was never around so the decisions didn't get made. There were, however, dozens of meetings and teleconferences with agendas and spreadsheets and discussion papers. The paperwork overwhelmed the decision making by a decisive margin. *The necessary logical compassion was nowhere to be found.*

Here was a high priced, well staffed human resources function, at the cutting edge of a massive corporate reorganization, entrusted with vital decisions to make for the future of the corporate entity – they labored in great numbers and produced a famine. I'm not demeaning their talents, they were a talented bunch, but this behavior resulted in their talents being wasted. On an organization chart, the executive looked like one of America's top human resources professionals. *His "it" was a disaster.*

Outing
I am still amazed at what pops out in the open all the time. I was once working as a host at a midtown Manhattan restaurant when one of the

regulars, who had had too much to drink, came over to me and began telling a story about Jews. I listened to the point where it became obvious that this was only going to be funny to anti-Semites. I stopped him abruptly and said, "You don't seem to realize, my Savior is Jewish." He stood there cold and silent. Through his fog (or his up until then latent unexpressed bigotry) he suddenly caught on that he'd made a major embarrassing mistake. He began to apologize. I interrupted him to say, "Please don't apologize but please don't speak like that in front of me again." For the next four years, every time he saw me in that restaurant (I was one of the co-owners), he tried to apologize again and again and again. I don't know if he learned his lesson to never let out what he knew in his heart was hateful, but he certainly remembered what I told him.

You know very well that a handful of people you will meet will try to sell you hate, stupidity, ignorance and just plain trash, and then tell you what they're selling is really candy. Intentionally ignorant people, people whose maturity and exposure to the world should make them know better but who chose to remain ignorant, and the unintentioned both must be stood up to and resisted. *When poison comes out in the open, you must counter it with the anti-venoms of faith, intelligence and logical compassion.* If a colleague at work displayed a photograph of Hitler or of an American bigot who praises Hitler, would you let that go unchallenged? While you likely won't change that person's opinions, you can and must force him or her to stick the garbage back into the closet. *Stand forthright, stick by your faith and values and live what you believe.*

Lesson:

In the 1830s, Nathaniel Hawthorne wrote a short story entitled *"The Minister's Black Veil."* The minister in the story showed up to deliver a sermon one Sunday wearing a piece of black crepe as a veil over his face. His neighbors and congregants were aghast – what was it that he's hiding, they asked among themselves. They speculated that whatever it was he was hiding had to be awful to cause this behavior in a clergyman. The minister continued to wear

his black veil until he was on his deathbed. In his final moments he was asked what sin had he been covering up for so long? His response was that everyone possessed some "hoarded iniquity of deed or thought." The question wasn't what had he been hiding, it was what had everyone else not faced in themselves.

Chapter Eight

The Law

From the late 1970s to the mid-1980s I worked for the Federal government in a number of positions within its General Services Administration, the agency that managed the government's buildings and properties. By the mid-1980s I was a senior management analyst working for the agency's executive managers, its Controller and Regional Administrator. I learned more about the worlds of business and work in this job than in any other. For the first time, I traveled through New York and New Jersey, meeting local leaders in whose communities government buildings were located. I met other Federal workers and got to know their jobs and working conditions. I participated in the planning for new and renovated government facilities and studied how these installations affected their inhabitants and the community around them. I performed a great deal of statistical collection, trend analysis and data extrapolation and then used that information to develop scenarios and recommendations for management improvements. When I started there, I was only a few months out of college, wet behind the ears but eager to build a career in public service. This was a major stop on my journey.

Toward the end of my tenure there, on a humid summer afternoon, with lunchtime past, in the office in lower Manhattan, the then Regional Controller walked out of his corner office. He stopped at his office door and surveyed the open work area. His secretary (that was a time before the terms "executive assistant" and "support staff" were in vogue) was not at her desk and not to be found. The other secretaries were missing in action as well. He cast his glance around the area, looked up at no one in particular and announced, "Where's the hen party?"

Protected Class Harassment
In 1986 the U.S. Supreme Court declared sexual harassment a form of discrimination prohibited by the Civil Rights Act of 1964. Title VII of that Act states,

"It shall be an unlawful employment practice for an employer ... to discriminate against any individual with respect to his compensation, terms, conditions, or privileges of employment, because of such individual's ... sex[.]"

Although Title VII applies to employers (with 15 or more employees for each workday in each of 20 or more calendar weeks) not individual managers, as agents of those employers our actions are the actions of our organizations. Moreover, individual managers may very well be held liable under applicable state statues and under civil and criminal laws for findings of harassment and discrimination.

The Meritor Savings Bank case was the landmark decision that opened the workplace door to the scrutiny of employees, the public, the courts, the legal profession, and regulatory organizations in the area of sexual discrimination. From that original case involving a female employee found to have been harassed by a male supervisor, the definitions of harassment have grown to include the treatment of certain protected classes.

Currently, these federally protected classes are

- People over the age of 40
- Gender
- Pregnancy
- Ethnic, national and racial groups (including skin color and citizenship)
- Religious affiliations
- Physical disability or condition (as defined by applicable law)
- Military status.

(Certain states and jurisdictions recognize additional protected classes, such as blindness, mental retardation and sexual orientation in Connecticut and genetic disorders in New York. Protection for these classes is provided under individual local statutes and often by the applicable state constitution. Although these classes are not recognized as protected by federal courts, within the respective jurisdictions, employers and managers are held to standards of compliance similar to those for Title VII protected classes.)

Harassment is any behavior or work environment that is reasonably perceived to be inappropriate, pervasive, severe and unwanted, that is based upon either a person's or persons' protected class. That behavior can involve men and men, women and women, men toward women, and women toward men. It can include any combination of work relationships: managers and workers, workers and other workers, managers and other managers, one on one, group on group, and a group and one person. It may involve reverse discrimination, where a member of what is defined as a "majority class" is harassed by a member of another protected class. (Remember that all classes, so-called "majority" and "minority," are protected.) A harasser can be a colleague, a customer, a contractor or a visitor. Harassment can occur either in the workplace or off-premises at an organization's sponsored event (holiday party, customer appreciation event, etc.) or at a non-sponsored event (colleagues get together after work for drinks).

Harassing behavior includes, but is not limited to -

- o Sexual advances, either overt or implied
- o Communicating sexually explicit or otherwise offensive language and gestures, such as jokes, comments and e-mail transmissions
- o Inappropriate and unwanted touching or other physical movements
- o Displaying photos, posters, drawings, cartoons, magazines, objects, calendars, mannequins and symbols of an offensive nature
- o Requests for sexual favors or attention that are unwanted and used as conditions of employment or advancement
- o Offensive behavior and work conditions that create an environment that is hostile to another employee's or other employees' ability to continue to work
- o Comments about a person's physical appearance or beliefs
- o Teasing based on a person's protected class characteristic(s)
- o Discussion about one's own or another person's sex life.

There are certainly other behaviors that belong on this list. Two general classifications exist for types of harassment: **quid pro quo** (Latin meaning "this for that") and *hostile work environment*. In the *quid pro quo* situations, the harassing party makes demands (usually romantic or sexual) of the party being harassed, in return for which either a positive employment action (promotion, travel opportunity, pay raise, etc.) will occur or a negative one (demotion, pay cut, lack of opportunity, dismissal, etc.) won't occur. Literally, this for that.

In instances of *hostile work environment*, the acts of harassment that occur are reasonably judged to prevent persons from performing their jobs and may be so severe as to force those affected to resign. A *hostile work environment* may be created by harassing or inappropriate conversations overheard by offended co-workers, the presence of graffiti and inappropriate materials in the workplace, and supervisors making harassing comments and threats that are unfulfilled.

In the U. S. Supreme Court decision in the case of Oncale v. Sundowner (in which the court first recognized same sex harassment), the court advised that Title VII is not a "general civility code," but that harassing behavior is "objectively offensive as to alter the conditions of . . . employment."

The landmark U.S. Supreme Court decisions of Ellerth and Faragher in 1998 established that employers could be held liable for the actions of their supervisors that create hostile work environments, where no tangible negative employment action has been taken against the complainant, even if the employer wasn't notified specifically of the harassment. The Court's message is managers must exercise "reasonable care" to know what is occurring in the workplace and to take appropriate action. **These two cases also establish a straightforward and strong defense for employers in these circumstances: have a clear anti-harassment policy, have an easy to use reporting process for complaints, and ensure managers and employees are fully aware of the policy and the process.**

You should keep in mind that neither the law nor an organization's policies can regulate employees' personal morality. As a manager and a leader, through your own conscience you are required to examine your own moral standards and how you present yourself at work, as we have discussed previously. *You are responsible for knowing and living your personal decency, respect and honesty in the workplace; treating others with awareness and respect; improving and maintaining a respectful and productive workplace to foster success for yourself, your colleagues and your organization; and, managing surely and fairly so that neither the law nor company policy nor your own code of decent conduct are undermined, ignored and destroyed.* You may well have teammates who are prejudiced against women (or blacks or Jews or white people or Muslims or . . .), and you may not know. And it may very well be that nothing you do, no motivation you exhibit, no behavior you model will change that twisted opinion. It is up to you to ensure that this hatred is *NEVER* voiced, expressed, acted upon or displayed at any time, anywhere even remotely involved with work. *PERIOD, FULL STOP.*

The courts in applying the law can and have, in certain circumstances and legal jurisdictions, found individual managers, like you and me, *personally liable* for causing or permitting harassment. This personal liability can include findings of guilt for civil assault and battery; intentional infliction of emotional distress; invasion of privacy; criminal liability; wrongful discharge; and more. It usually results in big bucks out of the manager's pocket.

Changes

I do believe that people can change. Change their hairstyle, their clothes, the way they do their work, their dedication, their energy, their attitude, even their beliefs. *I have faith that each of us has the power to make those changes and I pray for the insight and motivation necessary so that when those changes are needed, they can and do occur.*

As a manager, a teacher and a leader, you have the extraordinary opportunity and skill to assist your colleagues in making those changes. But in the end, neither you nor I can regulate what goes on inside the minds of our colleagues. *We do have the right, ability, authority and responsibility to ensure the workplace is free of all traces of fear, hatred, bigotry, prejudice and injustice.* That is what makes being a manager both difficult and rewarding. More is asked of a manager, spiritually, mentally and physically, and more is expected. This area of your duties, the ultimate safeguarding of the dignity of the workplace and your colleagues, is among the toughest and most sacred duties of all.

Why Do We Obey the Law?

The law exists to define the parameters and context in which we live. It is based upon standards of morality and practicality that we inherit from our forebearers and their experiences. U.S. law is a set of ideas, rules and hopes, based on the Founding Principles, descended from a Judeo-Christian heritage with major interpretations and contributions from other cultural sources, dating back to Greece, Rome, Egypt and beyond. There is room under the tent of this society for everyone who accepts the concept that living in civilization requires each of us to entrust our personal stake in maintaining peace, order and prosperity in a mutual agreement we call the Law. ***Our Rights come from our Creator.*** We are all equal under the Law – by our individual humanity, we each put the same stake in the process. When we are born or naturalized here, that stake is recognized. Even those who are neither born nor naturalized here but who live here are given some of the same rights and protections as the stakeholders.

This mutual agreement carries over into the workplace. When I conduct a daylong seminar on human resources issues for managers, I begin the section on the law by asking the participants, ***"Why do we follow the law?"*** The answers range from "Because it's the law!" to "Not following it leads to anarchy." The answers are all correct. We have a basic, core moral obligation to treat each other fairly and decently under the law. We have a legal obligation to obey the law. There are criminal penalties that attach to a number of these laws. We have a practical concern that lawlessness equals confusion and violence. We have a business prospective that potential and actual employees and customers will gravitate to an organization that operates in fairness under the law. We have a deeply personal commitment to treat others as we expect and require to be treated.

Since our Creator is the giver of our natural right to dignity, we obey Him by following laws that protect that dignity in and out of the workplace.

Almost thirty years ago, when I heard the boss ask about "the hen party," I had no idea his comment reflected an attitude that would become a potential violation of a law, without any thought that the Civil Rights Act of 1964 would be invoked. *I did know, instinctively, that what he said and why and how he said it were fundamentally wrong.*

In Clayton Buttram, Jr. et. al. v. United Parcel Service of America Inc., UPS paid $12.1 million in settlement for allegations that it did not adequately inform its part-time workers of African-American descent of chances and procedures for advancement at work.

In Kenney v. Wal-Mart Stores in Kansas City, Missouri, an employee alleged that her daughter-in-law, who was not a Wal-Mart employee, posted a notice on the company bulletin board stating that the employee's grandchild was abducted by the employee's son. There was no abduction; the son was late in returning the child to the mother. A jury found the notice to be libelous. Cost to the company for permitting it to be posted on its property, $426,000.

A Boston police officer of African-American heritage sued the city, alleging that the police department had taken more than a year to investigate an incident in which, he claimed, a white police officer had draped a noose over his motorcycle in the police garage. According to the white officer, it was a practical joke with no racist intent.

In Frederickson v. Olston Health Services, Inc. in Youngstown, Ohio, a 68 year old female who lost her job in a merger of two offices, alleged younger workers were given positions while she was forced into retirement. Company lost with a cost of $30.675 million.

When I ask why do we obey the law, I follow listening to the participants' answers by reading aloud cases like those. There is a bottom-line, dollars and cents reason for understanding and following the law. Data from the federal government's Equal Employment Opportunity Commission (the agency charged with enforcing anti-discrimination in the workplace laws) show that organizations lose 60 to 80% of discrimination lawsuits and that settlement of discrimination claims average $270,000.

 It is because of these reasons that I have always promoted the human resources function of an organization not as a cost center but as a cost savings and profit-contributing center. When the human resources aspects of the workplace are as second nature to managers as sales targets and productivity schedules, the positive interactions on the bottom-line are plain to see. Respected employees respect their employer. Employees who trust in their safety from harassment, discrimination and disrespect think, work, create, innovate and produce at far greater rates than their unsure counterparts. *Valued employees create value.* A lawful, respectful workplace attracts people; an unlawful, disrespectful workplace drives them away.

Where would you want to work?

> **"Take away my people, but leave my factories, and soon grass will grow on the factory floor. Take way my factories, but leave my people, and soon we will have a new and better factory." Andrew Carnegie**

> **"Trust is like the air we breathe. When it's present, nobody really notices. But when it's absent, everybody notices." Warren Buffet**

> **"The only irreplaceable capital an organization possesses is the knowledge and ability of its people." Andrew Carnegie**

There are many laws about which managers must have a working knowledge. I discuss harassment and discrimination regulations primarily because they involve some of the most common and thorny situations in the workplace for managers. Partnering with your organization's human resource and legal professionals, ensure that you have a complete knowledge of your organization's policies and a working knowledge of the key elements of the laws that most often touch the workplace – I provide a list of the key laws in the Appendix. If you work in a unionized workplace, have a thorough knowledge of the union contracts in force and a working knowledge of what are fair and unfair labor practices. Make sure your human resource professionals know that you need periodic updates whenever laws (both federal and local) affecting the workplace change.

The Law and the Bureaucracy
In the end, laws are administered by people. I've worked with government investigators and representatives whose professionalism and impartiality were unquestioned. Unfortunately, more than once in my career I've been nose to nose with agents of the government who took their job to be punishing companies and organizations because the complaining employee is always right, in their mind. These are dangerous folks. They think they hold the power of life and death in their hands – they can make the manager's life miserable enough so that organizations will do anything, including settling blatantly bogus claims of injustice, just to move on beyond the complaint situation. Organizations that settle for this reason quickly develop a reputation and become the deep pockets target for unscrupulous employees and their representatives.

I represented one firm, against whom the local human rights commission (acting on behalf of the EEOC) brought a harassment action based solely upon the employee's allegation that her manager gave her a "devilish" look (!). It is my experience that frivolous allegations like this are both permitted and given credence by a bureaucracy that is basically unwilling to use common business sense to weed out obvious nuisance complaints, for fear of offending employees.

117

The result of this lack of courage is businesses (and managers) being forced to defend themselves against the handful of dishonest employees who see bogus discrimination charges as tickets to quick, undeserved rewards. Unproductive, disruptive and hostile workers seek the cover of the law to unfairly protect themselves from being managed properly (and either straightening-up or shipping-out). Bureaucracy's negligence in this respect results in legitimate harassment and discrimination complaints (there are plenty that are of substance) being lumped in with and compared to the bad apples that are side by side in the barrel.

If your organization has done wrong by an employee, the most productive solution is to admit to it with the complainant and take all needed steps to remedy the particular situation and eliminate any re-occurrence. A justified apology goes a long way to healing a workplace wound and it costs less than legal wrangling. Backpay, training, a deserved promotion and proper counseling are all less expensive when undertaken by the organization before being ordered by a regulatory agency or a court or through a settlement agreement. In six years as the human resource leader for one of my employers, I settled exactly one claim – the manager involved had done wrong, big time wrong, and I knew it. I shortstopped other complaints by counseling the involved parties to speak together with my moderation and find a common solution. The remaining complaints I fought and the company prevailed in every one.

I once traveled to South Carolina to represent my company in an investigation by the EEOC of a pregnancy discrimination complaint. The complaining former employee had been away from work for a prolonged period of time. During her absence, managers handling her work came across dozens of open files and invoices that had not been processed and paid. There was over two months worth of work, undone and hidden in this employee's desk. The managers processed the work and confronted the employee with her unacceptable backlog when she returned. When she failed to bring her productivity and work product up to standard, allowing even more files to collect dust without telling management, she was fired. After being told she was dismissed, the then ex-employee announced, "I'm pregnant." Without her saying it, no one would have reasonably judged her condition just by observing her – the pregnancy was very early on and her absences had not been described as related to pregnancy. She made the dramatic announcement in a bid to find some protection in the law. You can't fire a person because that person is expecting a child. You can fire a person for not doing her work.

At my company's South Carolina office I met the local representative of the EEOC. She asked to examine certain employee records, the documentation of the undone work, and to question our employees and managers. During her questioning of our managers, I asserted the company's right for me to be present – she grumbled but acknowledged I could be present. When she finished her investigation, I sat down with her and our local manager.

The EEOC representative, in front of the manager, asked me a startling question, "Where are your people from?" She asked it in her mannered drawl. I knew exactly what she meant.

"I'm a New Yorker," I replied.

"No. I meant where do your people come from originally?"

"My family is originally from Virginia and the Carolinas," I countered. "Some of my ancestry is Native American, probably the Lumbee Tribe. In fact," I continued deliberately, "I was told that one of my direct relatives was once cornered by the Ku Klux Klan in his field. He had a shotgun with him so he took out three or four of them before they ran away." I watched her turn red in the face as I spoke.

"Oh. I see why you told me that story," she said.

She left the office shortly thereafter and the local manager asked me incredulously, "Why did you say that to her? Won't you hurt our case?"

I told the manager, the EEOC representative had already made up her mind that the company was guilty before she had conducted her investigation. The purpose of her questioning me about my "people" was to tell me that she, representing the EEOC and the government, was in the driver's seat in this situation. She was saying give up now because you're going back home but the decisions are going to be made here by her. She was a reverse bigot, using her prejudice to side with what she perceived as the underdog against the evil out of town company that fires pregnant women!

Sure enough, two weeks later the EEOC representative called me and said her findings were going to go against the company. When I asked on what she based her decision, she responded, "It's all over the port (where my company's offices were located) that your company discriminates." So hearsay and gossip were her sources. She asked me if I wanted to enter settlement talks now and avoid a protracted regulatory process. I responded, "No. The company is confident it did nothing wrong. We'll take our chances with your legal department."

"Okay. Have it your way," she replied.

I felt certain she was trying to push me to settle, so blinded by her anti-corporate prejudice that she didn't see the immense hole in her logic: no ethical EEOC lawyer would take a decision based on what's "all over the port" to a legal proceeding without hard evidence to prove the company was aware of the pregnancy prior to the firing and used the pregnancy as the motivation for the firing. One month later, I received the EEOC's official notice that its legal department declined to pursue the charge.

I had a similar experience with an EEOC investigator in Memphis who tried mightily to convince me that he was conducting a hearing and taking testimony when he was questioning my company's employees in our conference room. I told him that without swearing-in the employees under oath, taking a transcript of the questions and answers, and having the employees represented by counsel, there was no hearing and no testimony. Heck, you have to be given the opportunity to correct your sworn testimony even when you're legally deposed. This investigator also suffered from anti-corporate prejudice: the company was wrong because it was a company. The company also won that case.

It Begins Right Here, Right Now With You
Be aware that enforcing the law in the workplace, especially for alleged harassment and discrimination, starts with you as the manager. When you evaluate the circumstances of an allegation, remember it is the impact of the behavior, not the intent that determines its appropriateness and whether or not it is harassing or discriminatory. Harassment and discrimination erode the individual, the group and the organization in terms of productivity, morale and trust. ***Treat all complaints seriously and thoroughly.*** Always enlist the assistance and the advice of your human resources and legal professionals. Always document what is told to you and what you may uncover. Never wait to work on a complaint or try to bury it. In instances that do not rise to the level of prohibited behavior, such as one time events, document the situation and bring the parties together to resolve any problems, apologize and understand how to move forward to an appropriate working relationship.

What are the regulatory agencies and courts looking for when you investigate a complaint? ***They want to see (and your organization wants to conduct) an honest, thorough inquiry into the circumstances of the complaint.*** Don't deal with hearsay, gossip and rumors but do collect all the available information, speak to the parties and witnesses, and consider the sum of what is collected to make a valid determination. You can't resolve every complaint or know exactly what happened between two people with different and unsubstantiated stories. When the investigation is done, inform the parties, take necessary corrective and disciplinary actions, and follow-up diligently. What you may not have been able to uncover initially may rear its head again and present the organization with the evidence needed to understand and finally solve the problem.

A good indication of how seriously government takes its commitment to discovering and eradicating harassment and discrimination in the workplace is presented in the 2004 case of EEOC v. Sundance Rehabilitation. In the Sundance decision, the EEOC stated the public's best interests in finding and ending discrimination outweighed the private interests of employers who seek to buy terminated employees' waiver of their rights to file EEOC claims. Voluntary acceptance of monetary consideration can't trump the government's duty to address allegations of harassment and discrimination.

You are responsible for the following best practices -

- *Ensuring your organization's policies are known and followed.*
- *Ensuring your organization's complaint procedure is known and followed.*
- *Encouraging your colleagues to come forward with complaints.*
- *Demonstrating that you and your organization take all complaints seriously.*
- *Documenting actions you witness and statements made to you.*
- *Reporting all relevant information and complaints to the appropriate organizational element (usually human resources and legal).*
- *Discussing complaints and related information appropriately on a need to know basis only (generally with human resources, legal or higher management only).*
- *Being an active part of your organization's efforts to eliminate any harassment and discrimination in the workplace.*
- *Living and modeling the appropriate behavior.*
- *Disciplining violators of the organization's policies in accordance with the severity of their actions that are substantiated by an investigation.*
- *Ensuring there is no retaliation against a complainant, a witness or a target of a complaint.*
- *Assisting parties involved in a complaint, after the complaint is addressed to work together without animosity or retaliation. (This is particularly difficult and requires that you monitor the ongoing situation closely.)*
- *Taking all steps to make sure your workplace is in compliance with the letter and the spirit of the organization's policies. (Be especially aware of e-mails and Internet sites used by employees to transmit inappropriate images.)*

Our society has come a long way since the adoption of the modern era Civil Rights Act of 1964. That doesn't mean that some pockets of society have all caught up to where we should be now. Search your own heart – have you heard a remark that you should have acted upon immediately but didn't? Do you pass by conversations or materials that don't belong in the workplace but take no action? Relatively minor inappropriate behavior, using curse words or telling mildly offensive stories, left unchecked contribute to an environment of major inappropriate conditions. If you wouldn't want what you're about to say or do or what someone else is about to say or do, to happen in front of your mother, then it's likely you need to stop it before it goes any further in the workplace.

Not So Free to Speak
One misconception crops up at every place I work – the notion that employees have absolute First Amendment freedom of speech in the workplace and are therefore able and legally protected to say whatever they choose in the private sector environment. Wrong. The employer can set reasonable rules concerning speech in the workplace and these rules must be followed. You can wear a political campaign button on your jacket lapel outside the workplace but your employer can require you to remove it inside the office. The workplace is not a forum for political and social views that may be disruptive and contentious. With the motivation of having a harmonious and respectful workplace, the law supports organizations reasonably and justifiably modifying employee behavior at work to accomplish this. This does not mean that an organization may discriminate against or harass an employee because of his or her beliefs; organizations manage employees based on performance and behavior **in** the workplace.

Some time ago, the National Labor Relations Board reversed itself and returned to the old standard that only unionized employees were entitled to have a co-worker (usually a union representative or shop steward) present during investigative and disciplinary meetings. These rights to be represented (called Weingarten rights) had been extended to non-union employees. "Are you going to call me in to be disciplined? Wait, I want Carl in here with me."

Reversing that extension of Weingarten rights to the non-unionized workplace, the NLRB stated that "an employer's right to conduct prompt, efficient, thorough and confidential workplace investigations" was paramount to an employee's desire to have a co-worker present.

Day to Day

Organizations must take responsibility for training managers to understand laws affecting the workplace and how each manager adheres to those laws during the workday. *Obeying the law is not an extraordinary act.* It must be common practice in the workplace. In a decision, the Federal Circuit Court of Appeals ruled that organizations that don't train their managers to be aware of, understand and follow the law, are making an "extraordinary mistake." In this particular instance, Mathis v. Phillips Chevrolet, this mistake cost the employer $50,000. Several states now mandate that harassment training be given by the employer (or the employer's agent) to either all or to groups of employees on a regular basis. California requires employers of 50 or more people to deliver a minimum of two hours of harassment training to all supervisors every two years. Maine and Connecticut have similar laws. Don't wait for your locality to make it mandatory – harassment training, for managers and supervisors especially, is an investment in avoiding problems and developing awareness to catch potential problems.

Violence in the Workplace

In the last twenty-five years, a new and deadly phenomenon has entered the vocabulary of the workplace. This phenomenon is workplace violence. Workplace violence is the number one cause of workplace deaths for women and the number two cause for men. The U. S. Department of Labor and the National Institute for Occupational Safety and Health report on workplace violence. Here are some of the government's statistics:

- According to the Bureau of Labor Statistics' Census of Fatal Occupational Injuries, there were 11,613 workplace homicide victims between 1992 and 2006.
- This resulted in an average of just under 800 homicides per year.
- Half of U. S. employers with 1,000 or more employees had an incident of workplace violence in a 12-month period, reported as of October 2006.

- More than 70% of U. S. workplaces have no formal policy or program to address workplace violence.

Workplace violence is attempted, threatened or actual behavior that is intimidating or coercive or causes physical harm or property damage, on the organization's premises or during the performance of an employee's duties. This includes workplace bullying. The list of prohibited behaviors is a long one: using racial epithets, striking or trying to strike someone, sending a threatening message, pretending to have a weapon, bringing a weapon to the workplace, harming the organization's property or the property of a co-worker, stalking, and the like. Workplace violence sometimes overlaps with harassment and discrimination. I once investigated an incident in which a noose made of packing tape was affixed to the locker of an African American employee – workplace violence, harassment and a touch of discrimination.

Workplace violence doesn't pop up out of nowhere. The law firm of Littler Mendelson, pioneers in addressing this issue, lists thirteen early warning signs for the potential to commit acts of workplace violence.

1. **Direct or veiled threats of harm or intimidation of others.**
2. **An employee with a history of emotional problems. This is a difficult one to discern because of legal restraints on individuals' medical history, like HIPAA.**
3. **An employee's history of violent behavior. This is one of the most compelling reasons for managers to document complaint investigations and disciplinary actions – so that managers in the future have a record to reference.**
4. **The employee who can't take valid criticism of job performance; holds a grudge against a co-worker; or talks about the justification for harm coming to a co-worker.**
5. **All-consuming involvement with the job without any other apparent outside interests.**

6. **Loners who express a romantic interest in an uninterested co-worker. This can be discovered through sexual harassment investigations.**
7. **The employee who expresses extreme desperation over recent problems, such as divorce or loss of a job.**
8. **Carrying or pretending to carry a weapon to shock co-workers.**
9. **Expressions of fascination with weapons and the ability to harm others.**
10. **Expressions of fascination with reports of workplace violence, coupled with statements in sympathy or support of the perpetrators.**
11. **Showing disregard for the safety of co-workers.**
12. **Employees who perceive the whole world is against them.**
13. **An attitude of righteous indignation that the organization won't follow its own rules. This must be distinguished from employees who rightfully report possible lapses in following the organization's rules.**

Of paramount importance to you as a manager is to recognize these warning signs and enable the organization to address potential workplace violence problems before they become actual situations. Your organization must have a workplace violence policy. Like the absence of a code of conduct, not having this policy is an unacceptable and dangerous void. If a policy doesn't exist, lobby and work with human resources, legal counsel, and corporate security to put one in place. If one exists, read it, learn it, make your colleagues aware of it and have it posted prominently in the workplace. Review it at least annually with your team members. Be familiar with the warning signs so that you can separate unusual behaviors from threatening and potentially violent behaviors. Report any warning signs to the appropriate organizational element, in line with the policy. Make sure your organization and your team have a security plan that addresses where to go and what to do in case of a violent incident. Don't try to sweep warning signs and potential problems under the rug.

Don't -

*Soften a performance evaluation because you fear telling the truth and criticizing a colleague who exhibits warning signs will incite that person to violence. Working with human resources, your straightforwardness in an evaluation can uncover the latent problem and make the colleague realize that he or she needs further help, like an Employee Assistance Program intervention.

*Try to transfer or layoff a colleague exhibiting warning signs, in an effort to push away the problem. Many of the bloodiest workplace violence incidents of the last twenty years were preceded by just such an attempt. Deal with the problem as a current problem and enlist human resources to assist you in confronting the warning signs and talking with the troubled colleague.

Our colleagues are human beings who walk through that front door at work everyday. They bring their personal lives with them. Co-workers who are being stalked or harassed by a mate at home, have the same real fears at work. I assisted my company's Chicago office in helping a female employee whose common-law companion had turned violent toward to her. When she reported to her manager that she had been threatened, my office was called. I in turn called our corporate security manager. He interviewed the employee and her manager, then notified the local Chicago police. Having been in law enforcement, our security manager had instant credibility with the police. He spoke their language and knew what and what not to ask them to do. The local police stepped up their patrols of our local office's parking lot. They took a description of the harasser, his vehicle and his license plate number. A photograph of the harasser was posted in our local office's reception area, with instructions that if he was spotted the police were to be called and local management notified immediately. Local management provided escorts for our employee walking to her car after work. The harassment ended quickly and the harasser never trespassed the company's property. *All it took was for us to be serious, swift and resolute.*

Even when that particular employee went to work for another company in the industry, what do you think she said about our company?

Do the right thing and do it well – your faithful sense of self requires it.

Addressing the Issues

The ethical and legal disasters at Enron and WorldCom prompted the federal government to enact the Sarbanes-Oxley Act of 2002, followed by Dodd-Frank in 2010. As is the case in a number of other circumstances where outrageous and illegal conduct forces government's hand to answer with a new law quickly, Sarbanes-Oxley and Dodd-Frank are greatly flawed responses. But they are the laws with which we must live. The one provision that may affect you is the protections for whistleblowers. Employees of publicly traded companies who provide information that these employees reasonably believe relate to violations of securities laws or attempted fraud against shareholders, are protected from retaliatory acts. These information disclosures may be made to anyone with the authority to "investigate, discover or terminate (the) misconduct" alleged. Retaliation includes "interfering with the lawful livelihood or employment of any person" who blows the whistle, so it is very open-ended. The punishment is a fine and up to ten years in federal prison.

Consider that in terms of cases of employment discrimination reported to the EEOC alone, retaliation claims account for more than 27% (up from 15.3% in 1992) and are growing. Retaliation in any instance is ethically wrong, legally prohibited and just plain dumb. Retaliation almost always backfires with devastating results. Be aware that one of the most frequently overlooked retaliatory situations is the job reference. Some managers believe that once the employee is separated from the organization, that person is fair game for negative stories, gossip and retaliation when a prospective employer asks for a reference. Never give more information than a confirmation the person did work there, his or her title and final salary. No comments, hints, asides or warnings. Entrust all reference requests to human resources. In the case of Hillig v. Rumsfeld, a U.S. Circuit Court held that even though the separated employee had little chance of being hired by the new company, the negative reference by the previous employer had a "likely effect" on future opportunities and was probably retaliatory.

You will find that when you are looking into an employee complaint, you come across a colleague who may have important information as a witness but is him- or her- self unwilling to speak about it. This may be due to reluctance to implicate another co-worker, fear that speaking up will diminish the witness' ability to work with colleagues, or desire to "get past" an incident by ignoring it. Of course, none of these reasons will result in justice being done for either the organization or the colleagues involved in the complaint.

In fencing there is a concept called **"a choice in time."** This concept describes that point in a fencing match in which you realize your opponent has lost his or her will and is ready to be beaten.

In a complaint investigation, when you deal with a reluctant witness you will likely reach a choice in time. To do so and to take advantage of it, you must be listening with all your skills and relating authentically with the other person. If this is the case, you will see a choice in time in the colleague's eyes not wanting to focus on you and look into your eyes; in the way the colleague speaks in circles, talking about the future of everyone working together but refusing to discuss the facts of what did occur; the colleague's body language, shifting back and forth and turning away from facing you directly. Some seasoned investigators say a choice in time is indicated when a witness blinks excessively while talking.

Logical compassion requires you as a manager to pick up on these clues and acknowledge them. This is the time for you to emphasize that you are collecting information so that the organization can make a fair evaluation of a situation; you are not judging anyone, you're neutral. You should confirm the reluctant witness understands that your discussion is confidential on a strictly need to know basis. Re-affirm that the reluctant witness and you have the same goal: the best interests and well being of the organization that employs you both. Ensure that you make strong eye contact with the witness and use his or her first name. These techniques generally work but only when you are relating on an authentic and logically compassionate basis with your colleague.

Lesson:

"Today, our personal, corporate, political, and educational values are constantly challenged. The most successful leaders are those who respond to a changing world while staying true to what they stand for and aspire to accomplish. By doing so they ultimately create something of lasting value and significance that transcends the achievement of short term objectives. And they know what it is to inspire others to greatness." The Center for Values Based Leadership, Sacred Heart University

Chapter Nine

The Value of Values

How we see issues, subjects, events and other people is strongly influenced by our viewpoint. What we see is governed by how we look at it. Where we focus on a topic depends upon how we look at the subject matter. What we've seen helps determine how we will act. Motives rule behavior. And collective behavior, and the way that is managed, builds and re-builds culture.

The culture in some organizations pits value versus values: the bottom line on the profit and loss statement (or the top line, gross revenues) against the values of respect, honesty, fairness and faith. Is it okay to violate your values or the organization's values or your colleagues' values, in order to increase value? By ignoring values, can you really create value or can you create greater value by attending to values? Is there an inherent conflict between value creation and values? Are they mutually exclusive?

One aspect of life on which we can depend is constant change. The American philosopher (and former teamster) Eric Hoffer wrote a book about how difficult it is for us to accept and manage change. **He cited the "elements of fear" he felt when he changed from picking peas to picking string beans!**

Our surroundings change, although at times we don't notice. Yet, these changes around us affect how we go about our lives. If you work in a large city, do you take note of the buildings coming down and going up? The streets torn up and re-surfaced? The change in traffic patterns? The ever changing billboards for the latest fashions and television shows? More importantly, before you can manage it, are you looking for this constant change?

Value and culture change constantly. *Values are constant. Values apply in the midst of cultural change. Values lean to the compass needle of your faith; they are the deep roots that are nourished by your conscience.* No matter where or how your viewpoint and perspective change, values guide your motives and direct how you encounter and deal with change. *Values rule motives and motives rule behavior.*

> **"Everything has either a price or a dignity. Whatever has a price can be replaced by something else as its equivalent; on the other hand, whatever is above all price, and therefore admits of no equivalent, has a dignity." Immanuel Kant**

Your values are grounded in your faith. If your faith is material wealth, then your values will reflect maintaining and increasing your material status. Your lord will be money and the power and influence you believe money brings.

But if your faith is grounded in believing in your inner light, in a Creation for a purpose, in respect for yourself and your colleagues and in their dignity and importance, then your values will reflect your inborn ability to always strive to do what is right and to do good to be successful. *Your faith unlocks your talents for achievement and success.*

By reflecting these values in the workplace, you not only manage constant cultural change, you influence it. Organizations that put value in the values of honesty, respect and teamwork, have cultures that nurture and reward those values, and counter other values that are contrary and in conflict.

A "Great Workplace"

In 1999, Marcus Buckingham and Curt Coffman reported on a multi-year study done by the Gallup Organization to determine *"What is a Great Workplace?"* The definition used for "greatness" was employee satisfaction with their jobs and positive business outcomes. There were two significant discoveries in this study. **The first was "There are no great companies . . . only great workgroups."** This meant the responsibility for building and maintaining greatness and success at work rested squarely on the shoulders of managers. The second discovery was that there were twelve identifiable characteristics of "Great Workplaces." Here is the list:

1. **Employees know what is expected of them at work.**
2. **They have the materials and equipment needed to do their jobs right.**
3. **At work, they have the opportunity to do what they do best every day.**
4. **In any seven day period at work, they received recognition or praise for doing good work.**
5. **Their supervisor, manager or someone else at work seems to care about them as individual human beings, as persons.**
6. **There is someone at work who encourages their development.**
7. **At work, their opinions about work seem to count.**
8. **The mission or purpose of their organization makes them feel their jobs are important.**
9. **Their colleagues are committed to doing quality work.**
10. **They have "a best friend" at work.**
11. **In the last six months, someone at work has spoken with them about their progress on the job.**
12. **In the last year, they have had opportunities at work to learn and grow.**

That's the list. No single item is extraordinary in nature, in terms of complexity or potential to be managed fairly. Nothing jumps out as beyond the capability or capacity of any organization. You may well see your organization or an organization for which you worked, in one or more of these characteristics. *Like robust good health, you need the whole list in place to truly achieve greatness and maximum success.*

Reading these twelve sentences, is there any one that you can't implement? Taking into account now everything about which we've spoken so far, do you have the managerial tools to put this list into action? Remember the first discovery: there are no great organizations, only great workgroups. *You're not being asked to change the entire workplace culture, only that piece of it for which you are already responsible.*

You may work in an organizational culture that is contrary to every single item on this list. Why are you there, realizing this? I'm not being flippant – if an organization's culture is that de-humanizing (and I've worked for exactly one organization in my life that sank to that level), you need to get out as quickly as possible. Analyze your situation thoroughly, I'm not counseling you to up and quit. You may not be seeing the full picture because you need to change your viewpoint. Perhaps your enthusiasm for managing change and practicing your values have diminished and need to be re-awakened. Maybe that's why you're reading this book! You may not be taking ambiguous information into account. Never quit without checking your own viewpoint. The effort to make and manage cultural change is up to you as a manager, first. But if indeed your organization fails on every count, resists and punishes positive change, is based 100%, intractably on value with no room or acceptance of values, then that organization quit you a long time ago.

Do you think it is money that convinces people to stay in a job? It's certain that an organization must pay competitively to compete for and recruit talented people. How long can an organization hold and develop those talents if its values aren't competitive?

> **"People want to be paid well, but they won't stay at a company if they feel underappreciated or disrespected."**

Cross Border Culture Wars

You're probably wondering, do I have a story about culture and values? Well, yes I do.

I was given the task of arranging for an annual three-day conference for all of my human resources leader colleagues from around the world, to be held in the U.S. My team and I looked forward to showing our colleagues from abroad the same high level of hospitality and gracious welcome that they had shown us in previous years. We brainstormed about locations, agenda topics, accommodations, dinner parties, entertainment, gifts, the whole works. I reported to the U.S. General Counsel at the time and he gave me his full trust in making this event a success. He and I conferred with the global head of human resources in Switzerland, Sev. The General Counsel and I reported that we had tentatively secured a block of hotel reservations and meeting rooms with service at a midtown Manhattan hotel, with a large discount in price. In the presence of the General Counsel and me on the phone, Sev said "Yes. It sounds very good. Let's do it." My team and I went ahead, signed the hotel deal and solicited presentations from consultants and vendors on innovative topics and approaches in human resources. One vendor provided a block of seats at a Broadway play as a gift for the attendees. Our colleagues were flying in from Brazil, the Czech Republic, Germany, Italy, Switzerland, Austria, Norway, Great Britain and Singapore.

One week before the scheduled start, the General Counsel and I called Sev to re-cap the schedule and plans. It became clear that the Sev on this phone call was not the same one on the previous call. He interrupted my report to say, "We're not going to stay in a Manhattan hotel. The cost is too high." When I replied that not only was the cost at a deep discount that was very competitive with any price obtainable in the New York area, and the block of rooms contracted for, but he had approved the arrangement prior to it being finalized.

To back out now would entail significant penalties and leave us without a meeting venue and hotel rooms at the eleventh hour. Sev's reply was, "No. This company will never pay for a meeting in Manhattan." He then hung up the phone.

We scrambled to salvage the situation. The General Counsel appealed to our company president to argue the case for keeping the arrangements, with his counterparts in Switzerland. Failing that, the U.S. would not accept paying the penalties for canceling reservations that had been approved by Sev initially. After all, I had an attorney on both phone calls as a witness. My team and I shifted all the arrangements to a local hotel in Connecticut, near our office. Most of the vendor presentations had to be cancelled as well. The price we wound up paying for the local rooms was only marginally lower than the prices we had negotiated in Manhattan, and the revised arrangements provided a lot less convenience for travelers and for sightseeing, higher costs for transportation and fewer hotel amenities.

As it turned out, although we didn't hold the conference in Manhattan we didn't pay for the penalties – head office paid them. A somewhat more subdued meeting than the one originally planned and approved took place. One of the items on the agenda for the first day was a review of assessments of senior managers that had been performed by a well known German company. Sev posted copies of the assessments on an overhead projector for all of my human resources colleagues and me to read. The assessment of one Chinese manager of the company's pan-Asian business read, "Very intelligent for a Chinese." I literally gasped when I read that – I can't tell you what my foreign colleagues thought but my gasp was audible. I spoke up in measured tones, addressing Sev, the global human resources professional.

"The slide you just posted contains a sentence that talks about the ethnic characteristic of an employee and comments on that person's intelligence in a derogatory manner based upon his ethnicity. The employment laws in the U.S. are explicit about that type of statement, especially since this evaluation is being used to determine what his position with the company will be. Having made this statement now public, you need to consider the potential vulnerability it creates for the company concerning U.S. law."

I might as well have been speaking a dead language. The global human resources professional was baffled. He couldn't see my point. It was apparent that his global experience hadn't included learning the rudiments of U.S. employment law and practices. He asked me if he should continue showing the slides of the assessments. I advised him that in the best interests of the company, he should summarize the assessment findings in a brief talk and not show any others. He complied, not reluctantly by the way but in a resigned fashion that indicated he didn't see what all the fuss was about. At a subsequent meeting with us, he remarked about a senior manager from Holland, "He's stubborn but then what do you expect from a Dutchman?"

On the second day of the meeting in the U.S., Sev distributed copies of the final draft of a booklet intended to be distributed, in English, worldwide to every company employee (there were tens of thousands of employees globally, with workers on every continent, even Antarctica).

The booklet's purpose was to introduce the new global nature of the company and revise the prevailing corporate culture to build an international reputation among all employees. I looked through my copy – it was a professionally prepared publication, on expensive paper, in full color with a durable binding. Unfortunately, it had one major flaw. I raised my hand to be acknowledged by Sev and said, "This is an attractive employee relations tool but everyone pictured in it, and there are a lot of people pictured, look exactly the same." Again, I could have been speaking a dead language. Sev gave a blank look – I think he was saying to himself "this guy is a royal pain." My General Counsel, who was attending, broke the silence by commenting, "Tony is right. This won't be very useful for building a global identity with U.S. workers without some representation of the variety of people who already work for us." This didn't seem to sink in with Sev either. He mumbled that he would take the issue up with the communications staff back at headquarters and then asked for the copies to be passed back to him.

The General Counsel told me later that after the day's session adjourned, Sev approached him and asked, "Do you think Mr. Shaw was really upset by the booklet?" Sev just didn't get it. His actions and comments illustrated a blindness to cultural values other than his own and an ignorance of the value of an inclusive culture.

He didn't understand that cultures change as you cross borders and expand your horizons. He didn't value the inherent dignity of all of his colleagues, especially the ones who were culturally different from him. That he was in the most senior human resources leadership role for an enormous global organization, was frightening. How could his company expect him to support, counsel and guide values-based management when he lacked understanding of the value of values? He was fighting a culture war within himself. I don't know the outcome of that war because he and the company parted ways about six months after that conference.

It Isn't Rocket Science

My friend and colleague Al Pettenato told me, "The freight business is very simple – we buy space on planes, ships and trucks at one price and we sell that space to our customers at a higher price the customers are willing to pay. We get the higher price because we deliver a service that meets the customers' needs. This is not rocket science!" He is right. ***Organizations thrive and are successful when they meet and exceed the needs of their customers.*** Organizations require the ability to relate to, understand and anticipate those needs. Organizations must have the depth of talent to create solutions for customer needs. Customers want their needs met by organizations represented by employees who understand, listen to and respect them, and who are responsive to their needs, all at a fair price. Is it really more complicated than that?

- o ***Who are your organization's customers?***
- o ***Who will be your customers?***
- o ***What does your workforce really look like?***
- o ***From where will your future employees come?***

And adhering to your values as you manage change and maintain a culture of respect, also isn't rocket science. An organizational culture of values and respect doesn't just refer to tolerance or acceptance of people other than you. Such a culture has as its basis an understanding that your viewpoint of the world ought to be greater than what you can see and have seen. ***This culture speaks of a world filled with texture and color, the music of human aspiration and the energy of human dignity***.

Where I once lived, early each morning Sunday through Saturday dozens of men gather near the train station and wait. They wait for employers driving in work trucks and pick-ups to stop at these designated places and hire them for day labor. These men who are waiting aren't bums or lowlifes or hustlers. The overwhelming majority are hardworking breadwinners for their families. They are human beings who perform

138

work that would cripple most people I know – and they work for wages far below what you or I would probably accept. By waiting in all sorts of weather and conditions, they've made a moral choice to pursue hard work to make a living, rather than crime or the public dole. Their children look like my children. I know that these men have the same prayers and hopes for their families that I have for mine.

One of the greatest strengths of the American culture is that nowhere else in the world would these men go willingly and labor as they do, in their desire to build a future for their families. *It is my belief that inside and outside the workplace, our culture is and must be compassionate enough to deal with issues of great sensitivity and complexity without forgetting the essential humanity of those involved.*

Organizational culture encompasses more than considerations of nationality and ethnicity. Cultural differences are often about perceptions in the workplace, rather than speaking different languages or hailing from different countries. One commentator, Harry Brull, Senior Vice President at Personnel Decisions International, composed an intriguing list of what he saw as the essential elements of organizational culture.

- o **How a company wants to be perceived.**
- o **How employees treat each other.**
- o **How employees deal with time.**
- o **What operational factors have priority.**
- o **Who the heroes have been.**
- o **How good or bad behavior is acknowledged.**

Brull cautions that the senior leadership of any organization doesn't have the greatest influence on determining the perception of the culture: employees' peers and managers do. What managers say and do show colleagues what the culture will accept and reward.

Shortly after the start of a corporate integration of two companies, I was asked by my CEO to go to Chicago to troubleshoot employee complaints coming out of two offices there, one each from the two predecessor companies. These two offices were in the process of being combined but without any job losses because they serviced different types of customers. One office managed the accounts of large multi-national corporations and the other cared for small and medium-sized businesses.

The combined office would be located in one building, with enough room for both sets of employees to work and become one force. The larger office would receive the colleagues from the smaller installation – everyone would have to get used to sitting and working side-by-side.

In anticipation of this combination, the larger office staged a "Welcome Day" for their new colleagues from the smaller office to come visit their new workplace and meet their new co-workers. The welcoming office prepared food and decorations. On the scheduled day, about half of the re-locating employees arrived and took part in the event. It was after this that the complaints started to reach my office and the CEO. Both offices observed, separately, that they could not work with the other office. The "Welcome Day" was an insult to the arriving office because it demonstrated the receiving office's condescension and for the receiving office, the arrivals' lack of participation and unfriendliness were signs of hostility!

When I sat with the employees in each of the two offices, something interesting emerged as I listened. Each group expressed its singular pride in *how* its work was accomplished. The folks managing large customers segmented the tasks of servicing their customers, handing off their specialized work products (completed customs processing, certified airway bills, computerized tracking and tracing, etc.) to each consecutive work group, so that quality customer service was the sum of individual group efforts. The office managing small to medium customers, took practical responsibility and care for every aspect of their customers' service. One office was a set of specialized work subgroups; the other was a unified team of generalists.

Do you know what the common core gripe of each office was? "They (the other office) can't tell me how to do my work!" They were two distinct work cultures based upon each culture's method of getting the job done, born out of the work requirements of two distinctly different types of customers. And the cultural clash of trying to put these two cultures not just side by side but blended together at work, was very real and initially very invisible to management.

"You change culture by giving people new tools that actually work."

After many years of giving seminars on organizational culture and diversity in the workplace and investigating complaints, I've come to two distinct conclusions:

1. All organizations each have many different internal cultures.
2. As many individual human beings who are alive in the world, that is the number of diverse cultures with whom we must potentially work and relate.

In addition to your managerial toolset of faith, logical compassion, empathic listening, leadership skills, authenticity, respect and best practices, managing cultural differences requires a healthy dose of patience.

> *Patience is the tool when reflection is required, rather than hasty reaction.*

Ambiguity abounds in cultural issues, so organize yourself to look and be ready for conflicting opinions and information. Cultural issues, more so than most other workplace conflicts, tend to generate sharp distinctions about what is perceived to be right (specialists' work) and what is seen as clearly wrong (generalists' work, and vice versa). Remember, however, that first you must come to understanding cultural differences (and conflicts) with your authentic self, prepared to listen reflectively with an open mind and heart.

Culture changes when you motivate its inhabitants positively to change.

Gossip

A few words about gossip. Gossip can wreck a workplace, especially if office gossip is an ingrained part of the work culture. It is an old cultural tool that always fails. Listening to gossip is seductive – the more you hear, the more you want to pass on to the next person and discover what he or she has heard. In workplaces in which the organization's commitment to keeping its people informed is weak or non-existent, gossip fills the information void in the culture. No matter what the intentions of the gossiper, gossip is always a negative element. *It must not be permitted to replace the truth and poison the culture.*

The truth is a powerful best practice tool. Use it. We are more fearful of what we think we don't know than we are of "bad news" communicated truthfully and clearly.

To combat gossip's effects in the workplace culture successfully, your organization, through you, must make it clear that gossiping is unacceptable. You don't invite it, listen to it, pass it on, and most importantly don't use it in your decisionmaking. Never base a disciplinary action or other decision at work on secondhand stories where you cannot go to the firsthand sources for direct confirmation. Your organization's policies must state that gossiping in the workplace is prohibited and will be grounds for appropriate discipline. When gossip comes your way, deal with it immediately; confront the gossiper, question the validity of the story, determine the source, confront the source in the company of the gossiper, straighten out the information, and apply discipline. The serial gossiper must be told a repeat incidence will result in his or her being disciplined, up to and including termination.

"Gossip is the Devil's radio." George Harrison

Proactively, as a leader you must keep your teammates well informed about the organization's business, status and plans as you become aware. You must prompt your managers to keep you informed. *You must demonstrate your commitment to a work culture that puts its value in supporting an intelligent, experienced and involved workforce. You must reinforce these tools. You must live your faith.*

Lesson:

"Buy the truth and do not sell it; get wisdom, discipline and understanding." *Proverbs 23:23*

Chapter Ten

Work, Life Best Practices

Managers are active, not passive, beings. We see what is going on around us – we have to see around corners at times! We sense the workplace mood. We hear what our colleagues are saying to us and among each other. And we must separate the useless information from the useful quickly. Our brains must work on foreground and background, attentive to every clue and nuance, utilizing what we learn that is of immediate value, dumping the junk, and storing the intelligence we gather for future use.

Using that information, there are fundamental work tasks we all perform as managers.

- Interviewing job candidates
- Assigning work
- Recognizing and promoting employees
- Coaching, counseling and disciplining
- Evaluating job performance
- Separating employees from organizations.

Our colleagues move through our teams and organizations in many directions, led by us. For us to succeed in leading them requires our committed application of the full complement of our natural management skills. The measure of our faith, in a Creation for a purpose, in the worth of others and in ourselves, will be taken as we perform these tasks.

As the leader, it is your responsibility to achieve the maximum success for your team, your organization, your colleagues with whom you share these tasks, and yourself, as you encounter and manage these situations. It is paramount for your successful efforts in each instance, to appreciate that there can be positive good that accrues from the most seemingly negative of these tasks. ***Your soul demands nothing less.***

No logically compassionate manager takes pleasure in firing a person but, managed successfully with faith, a job separation will benefit all parties. I remember my former colleagues who later in their work lives told me being fired was one of the best things that happened to them. I've experienced voluntarily leaving an executive position with a large company because I couldn't re-locate away from my family. Although this wasn't managed in an authentic, respectful and logically compassionate way, the outcome for me was eventually very positive. I can only speculate (but with a firm belief that my speculation is correct) that had the managers with whom I dealt in my personal situation been men and women guided more by faith than by value, they too would have been motivated to see and act on how this separation could have better served their organization and the lives of everyone involved.

It is much worse as a manager to be motivated (really, unmotivated) by lethargy, complacency and a lack of caring, than to be driven to intentionally do harm in these instances. That colleague on the other side of the situation can see and deal with the purposefully hurtful manager; the unmotivated, neglectful manager is an amorphous target, difficult to focus on and harder to counter. The negative presence shows itself for what it is but negligence pretends to be neutral.

> **"A different world cannot be built by indifferent people."** *Saint of the Day* **June 6th**

When you take care with the lives of your colleagues, you take care with your own humanity in the workplace, a humanity given by our Creator.

Hiring and Promotion

Before you fill a vacancy on your team, you need to consider and answer a series of questions, in cooperation with fellow managers, human resources and your teammates.

- o Why is this position vacant? What did the previous incumbent do or not do that resulted in this vacancy?

- o Does my team still need this position? What does it contribute to meeting our goals? How has it achieved or not achieved that contribution?
- o Is this position still funded in the budget? Can my team meet its goals without this position? Can I use budgeted funds to achieve a more important goal?
- o Has this position's role or duties changed since it was last filled? Is the position description up to date and accurate? Is the current salary at market level?
- o What was the feedback from the previous incumbent through the exit interview?
- o How can human resources assist me in reviewing this position, revising the position description, updating the salary and compensation, and broadening the recruiting effort to achieve a successful hire?
- o As an organization, are we reaching out to all the available sources to find the best qualified pool of candidates?
- o Remember **"in a broad sense, hiring policies . . . ultimately concern the management of risk." (El v. SEPTA, 2007)**

Once you have tackled and answered these questions, you are ready to start the recruiting process. You and your teammates may be aware of professional groups, forums, publications and other competitors where qualified candidates are likely to be either present, known or reachable. The recruitment process is a collaboration between you and human resources, therefore the exchange of useful information, observations, research and hints must be active and thorough. The success or failure of recruiting is a joint responsibility: intensive cooperation with human resources improves the chances of finding the best possible candidate immeasurably. ***When you have prepared this strategic foundation for each recruiting effort, you have set the stage for productive interviews that lead to a successful, productive hire.***

Take care when interviewing prospective candidates that you keep the best interests of the organization and of the applicant in mind. Never reveal or discuss your hiring decision with an applicant, even if that person is the one you think you want to hire. The background check and drug screen might uncover information that can change your mind. A statement by you that can be reasonably perceived by the applicant as a promise of employment may have serious legal consequences. This rule governs in promotion situations as well. Moreover, you can cause applicants to believe a job offer is guaranteed, raising their hopes, and putting the organization's reputation in jeopardy when another candidate is selected. Don't discuss or promise perks, rewards, or opportunities that will be extraordinary and out of line with the general compensation package of your organization, unless you are completely sure that these benefits will be delivered. Just because the promise isn't in writing, doesn't mean it can't be legally actionable by a subsequently disgruntled or non-performing employee. Keep your remarks neutral when talking with candidates for hire or promotion. Let human resources check references and deliver the hiring offer.

Do, however, conduct a hiring or promotion interview with the clear intent to develop a full picture of the candidate's qualifications, enthusiasm and personal style. Be aware of your listening skills, especially the flood of information that occurs before you start the conversation. Prepare yourself. Read the resume and application or the personnel file thoroughly, several hours or the day before the interview. Make pre-notes of what you want to ask, areas that seem unclear from the record, the candidate's thoughts on performance issues and so forth. Don't go in to conduct an interview cold. It doesn't work. You can't ask valid questions and take in the needed information if you are reading the resume while you say "hello."

Through preparation you know what will be required of the candidate in the job or the new position. Ask for examples of how the candidate has utilized or learned each of the required skills and abilities. Remind yourself about "Who, What, Where, When, Why and How" to ensure you use open-ended questions that solicit the maximum useful information. It is a best practice to ask prospective hires their reasons for each job change during their careers. Of course, there are questions and areas that you must avoid. Here is the best list of "10 areas of questions to avoid in job interviews" that I've ever seen –

1. **Are you married? Divorced?**
2. **If you're single, are you living with anyone?**
3. **Do you have children? How many? How old are they?**
4. **Do you own or rent your home?**
5. **What church do you attend?**
6. **Do you have any debts?**
7. **Do you belong to any social or political organizations?**
8. **Do you suffer from an illness or disability?**
9. **Do you plan to get married, start a family?**
10. **What would you do if your spouse was transferred?**

I'd add don't question female applicants about child care arrangements or their feelings about working with and managing men. These are all landmines in the field of employment law and any one of these questions or areas of improper inquiry can and often do result in blowing up into complaints and legal actions. Your aim is to gather enough information to judge the prospect's job performance qualifications. The interview is not a social chat. If the candidate provides information in one of these forbidden areas without your asking, move on to your next question without commenting or following up on the out of bounds topic.

During the interview you are trying to develop a full picture of who this candidate is. How is the person dressed, is it appropriate for the interview, neat and clean? Is the person adequately groomed – be careful not to judge ethnic or racial factors such as the stubble some African American males can develop from shaving, or the fact that in certain cultures, males are forbidden from cutting their facial hair. Does the person speak and act in a self-respecting and a respectful manner? Is the candidate a good listener and a thoughtful speaker? Did the candidate come to the interview prepared? Did he or she ask relevant and considered questions? Did he or she maintain eye contact while speaking? Maintain proper posture? Display common business courtesy in language and actions? Demonstrate an enthusiasm for the opportunity? Display an understanding of the job and the organization? Evidence a commitment to grow in the position and the organization? These are all relevant observations you need to make. ***The best practice, proactive process to avoid workplace problems begins at the first recruitment through to the job interview.***

Orientation

Once hired, after a successful background and drug screen, the new employee needs to be introduced and brought into the organization's culture quickly. Along with the requisite paperwork and forms, he or she needs to be given a copy of the Employee Handbook of your organization's policies: ensure you receive a signed acknowledgement of receipt that becomes part of the new employee's personnel file. Assign the new employee to a co-worker in the team who will be available to answer the newcomer's questions, be a guide through the work area and the management structure, follow up during the first few days, and be a familiar face in a new place. You need to follow up with both the newcomer and the assigned co-worker to judge how well this orientation period is progressing and if additional steps or resources are necessary to achieve a full integration into the work group and the organizational culture.

It is a best practice to have an orientation session for new employees, preferably in a group setting during the first two weeks on the job, led by your organization's human resource function. There, newcomers can get to see one another and share questions. Orientation sessions usually introduce the organization's purpose statement and history, highlights in the employee handbook, the benefits program, an overview of the performance evaluation process, and elements of the workplace culture and structure. These sessions re-enforce the organization's demonstrated commitment to make the hiring decision a successful one. A new employee's first weeks in a job are critical in setting the tone for that person's work life in your organization. As the manager, you need to ensure that this person is welcomed and supported during this vital period, through collegial interaction. The workplace is a living space for eight or more hours of most employees' lives, five or more days a week.

Do not consider a probation period a safety zone for firing newly hired employees. In legal reality, such a period is not a safety zone where the organization can sever the employment relationship without presenting a reasonable cause. Remember, the doctrine of *employment-at-will* is limited in its application. You always need a reasonable, documented cause for terminating an employee – do not rely solely on ***employment-at-will***.

The employee may resign at any time but your job as the manager is to not lose a valued teammate for frivolous or actionable reasons. One of the basic benefits of assigning a co-worker to a new employee during the first three to four weeks is to head-off such surprise terminations. A new hire represents a significant cost to the organization; if you lose that person before you recoup that investment, which is both a human and a financial loss, you decrease the bottom-line. A probation period sets up a false sense of security on both sides.

What ***assures*** new employees most about their place in the organization is what ***re-assures*** current employees: you are wanted and respected, your skills are valued, you have an important role in producing our product, you will know what the organization expects of you and how you will be evaluated, you will have the resources to get your job done, you will be told how you are doing and where you need to improve, and you will be recognized and rewarded for your achievements and ideas. ***Building the basis for a work relationship of trust and respect is no more complicated than that***.

Your organization must strive to be an employer of choice. This means building a workplace culture that draws talented people to your organization, keeps them, develops and promotes them, and rewards them for their contributions to enhancing the organization's value. Your organization must be known throughout its market sector as a place people want to join.

You, your colleagues and even your former colleagues spread this message by word of mouth. ***This is your organization's reputation and it is established and maintained one employee at a time.*** This is where people give their best and want to stay – the retention rate is high and the turnover rate is low, employee development that leads to promotion is the preferred method of filling vacancies, and employee satisfaction surveys document positive morale and ambitious expectations. Customers expect and receive superior service.

This not a perfect place. Problems arise and some people are at odds or unsatisfied with their work situations. Market demands mean changing organizational needs and new challenges. No organization can always be ahead of the curve and totally prescient about employee attitudes. It isn't a problem-free, unchallenged organization for which you strive – it is a workplace culture that tackles problems and challenges with honesty, clarity, respect and logical compassion. *The organization that rallies its troops with wisdom and speed meets its challenges and resolves its problems effectively, without harming productivity or reputation.*

Performance Evaluation

Business plans must be linked to employee development and a fair rewards strategy. Performance evaluation and the development of employees' skills and jobs are as important elements of your organization's planning as production goals and profit margins. Your organization's evaluation and development plans and processes must support a workplace culture based on challenging employees to grow beyond where they think they are capable of growing. The organization's criteria for success and requirements for rewards must be linked directly to performance evaluation and employee development.

As a manager, you are the critical factor in evaluation and development. You,

- o *Articulate your team's purpose and plans within the framework of the organization's goals*
- o *Set the challenges*
- o *Maintain a respectful workplace that is safe but challenging!*
- o *Support, understand and appreciate your team and their efforts*
- o *Coach and counsel teammates in their achievement of their goals*
- o *Ensure each teammate knows his or her individual responsibilities and role in meeting the organization's goals*
- o *Manage a compensation and reward structure that is easily understood, adhered to and credible.*

(Few organizational mistakes are more certainly fatal to credibility and reputation than reneging on a merit based rewards structure. Organizations that make this mistake experience employee disillusionment, resentment and revenge. Don't do it.)

I've been part of a variety of performance evaluation processes. Many were inadequate, antiquated, not user friendly and consequently largely ignored. Managers regarded them as a waste of time, nothing more than useless filler for a personnel file. These managers were always late in completing the process and turning in the paperwork to human resources, who barely gave the forms a once over before filing them away forever.

Employees knew nothing real and tangible ever came of these evaluations – no plans for skills improvement, no change in compensation that reflected actual performance, and no acknowledgement by the organization that the evaluations meant something to managers or were utilized in a strategic way for the business. These instances were more harmful to the organization's growth and progress than if there was no evaluation process in place at all.

I've participated in, managed and helped create performance evaluation processes that were lively, vital, integral parts of the workplace culture, useful to management and employees, and the source of a tremendous amount of strategic information that could be put to use in the organization's planning. *A viable performance evaluation process is a powerful best practice tool for building organizational values.*

Although these processes differed in how they looked and how they were conducted, they all had certain best practice elements in common:

- They were based upon the principle that each employee was an important part of the organization's capacity to meet its goals, sustain its existence, improve its market position and grow.
- These processes acknowledged that each employee contributed to the bottom-line, therefore, each employee was more than just a brick in the organization's foundation – each employee was a profit center.
- These two messages were stated upfront in the evaluation processes and used as the first elements of the processes that

were communicated to the employees. Namely, "You are a valued part of our organization's creation of value. Without you, we don't exist."

- The introduction and training for these processes were given to the managers first, recognizing that their commitment and understanding were necessary for the processes to be implemented and used successfully. Any issues about the processes that arose from the managers' training were addressed swiftly and changes were made before the processes were rolled out to employees.

- Significant training time for the processes was dedicated for all employee groups. The message was clear that evaluations were important and serious and the organization was making an investment in doing this correctly.

- Any employee questions, issues or concerns from the training sessions were addressed promptly, right back to the employee from human resources and the appropriate manager.

- While the processes were annual, the emphasis to managers and employees was on continual performance review and evaluation as a regular part of the workplace duties. Managers were instructed to hold at least two performance review sessions per employee per year, with more frequent meetings if needed. Managers and employees were told that performance evaluation was an ongoing dialogue and the proposed evaluation plan for each person was the basic document for that dialogue.

- Performance evaluation plans were signed agreements between the employee and the manager. Rather than the old method of having the manager write the plan and the employee agree to it, the employee drafted the proposed plan and met with the manager to discuss it and come to a mutually agreeable plan. That agreed upon plan was then signed by both.

- The agreed upon performance evaluation plans contained discrete factors for measuring the most important, currently relevant elements of the job and the expected outcomes. For example, a production supervisor would agree with her manager that she would implement a new work routine by the first quarter of the year (one factor in the evaluation) that would result in increasing productivity by 10% (another factor). In this way, the parties understood that performance of certain job elements were worth measuring, and could be measured by both general completion and quantifiable achievements. These processes specifically avoided trying to measure every aspect of a job because that was impractical and not user friendly. Colleagues would use the processes only if they knew they were easy and practical.

- The individual plans each contained a short statement of the employee's job description. This documented an agreement between employee and manager of what each person's role was in the organization.

- The processes allowed managers and employees to change the evaluation elements by mutual agreement if circumstances of the job changed during the year.

- Part of the evaluation elements were behavioral factors that were linked to the organization's statement of purpose. These factors included "Promotes teamwork," "Maintains a respectful relationship with co-workers," etc. This recognized that soft skills (listening, respect, leadership) were as important to the organization, the team and the individual as hard skills (cost savings, productivity, profit margin).

- The signed performance evaluation agreement document was kept, as a physical copy, by both the employee and the manager as a reference tool. Both parties were encouraged to review the document regularly, in addition to the periodic face-to-face reviews.

- The processes set forth calendars for completion of each step: drafting the plan, signing it, periodic face-to-face reviews, final review, signed agreement on final ratings. Everyone was held to those deadlines.

- When an employee and manager could not reach a signed agreement on the final ratings at the end of the year, their dispute was referred to a separate resolution process with the manager's manager, the next higher level of authority. The more senior manager was charged with reviewing the dispute, researching relevant data and records, and resolving the final rating.

- Employees were encouraged to write their responses in the final review document, which would become permanent parts of the evaluation record.
- Employee development plans were included in the final signed document.
- A reward program, separate from the compensation system, was built into the processes so that a designated defined level of superior performance triggered a payout. This payout accounted for individual performance; another part of the reward program accounted for sharing the organization's success for the year if certain overall targets were met and the employee attained a designated final rating (generally "met all expectations" or better).
- The final signed evaluation documents were reviewed individually by human resources for quality control, tracking and implementation of development plans. Human resources also monitored and analyzed trends in the processes; Were employees of certain managers experiencing similar performance problems? Did some managers have evaluation disputes with a number of employees? How did the ratings trend for different teams?

Development

Employee development is not training. It is much more. It is ongoing. It is interactive. It is daily. It is not bound to a classroom. *It is dynamic.* It is required constantly, across the board, up and down the ladder of the organization's structure.

Every employee needs to develop underutilized and unrecognized skills; learn new skills; sharpen the focus on current skills; and stay up to date on the ever changing nature of business, people and management. CEOs need employee development as much as file clerks. Most CEOs I've known have needed development in the area of people management skills significantly more than most file clerks with whom I've been blessed to work.

Employee development covers such a wide range of available techniques, settings, methods of delivery, and topics that a successful, best practices-focused organization must have a chief development officer (who might have the title of Training Director, Head of Training and Development, or Vice President of People Development, among others). Every organization in which I've worked has had a Chief Financial Officer to set financial policy and manage the monetary assets; employee development is the human side of the investment function.

Providing employees with a variety of opportunities for development is an investment in enhancing their skills, your team's capabilities, and the organization's workforce quality. There is another, more subtle dividend that accrues from this – employees feel and see themselves as respected, important, valued and recognized. Employees who experience a range of development opportunities are more loyal to their organization, less likely to leave because of material enticements from elsewhere, and better equipped to face new challenges. The work culture that offers and promotes development is exciting and magnetic, attracting, retaining and elevating employees who look forward to participating in it every workday. *Development opportunities are actually part of the organization's best practice recognition efforts.*

Employee development can occur throughout the workday, in a variety of ways to spark the interests of the diverse spectrum of your colleagues (and your own interests). Too many organizations pigeonhole development as classroom training, which leads to the misperception of it being tedious hours spent in a stuffy room listening to a boring lecture or watching a video, while participants barely stay awake. Best practices include:

> *Every organization should consider implementing a tuition assistance or reimbursement program for employees. Where this is financially possible, organizations should acknowledge and support the ambitions of colleagues who make the effort to further their educations. The cost of courses taken in subjects that relate to the organization's business should be covered (if passed) by a program open to all employees. On-line and distance learning courses*

should be covered, with proper human resources review and management approval prior to instruction. Some organizations also cover the costs of books and instructional materials. These benefits are generally taxable for the employee.

Meet with your team on a regular basis (weekly or more frequently) to discuss current information about your organization's operations, the industry and any updates that affect them. Open up the floor to allow teammates to discuss issues and concerns, and ask questions. These meetings are the most effective forums for disseminating organizational news, including customer issues, new work rules and re-structuring projects.

On an annual basis or more frequently, review your organization's policies that are part of maintaining a respectful workplace – anti-harassment, discrimination and violence in the workplace prohibitions, alcohol and drug use rules, code of conduct, use of the internet, etc. Workplace safety rules should also be reviewed periodically. These policy refresher sessions serve to remind colleagues of what is expected of them in the workplace and inform you of potential areas of concern.

These suggested approaches are in addition to formal training and development opportunities managed by your organization's head of employee development. These formal programs need to be branded; presented as a formal curriculum that is designed with the input of employees and management, and shown as the nucleus of an in-house advanced educational facility. This curriculum should be revised annually, with details about course content, prerequisites and intended participants published in a print or on-line schedule.

Best practice employee development programs function and are identified as organizational institutes of advanced learning, graduating employees for higher purposes within the framework of the overall strategic plans.

Employee development must be done on a planned basis for each employee. The previous year's individual performance evaluation becomes the blueprint for development decisions. New and additional development opportunities are included in individual development plans as these plans are implemented throughout the year.

Succession Planning

Succession planning is an important best practice element of the employee development process. Frankly, I'm baffled by the number of organizations I've encountered, managed by intelligent people, where succession planning not only isn't done, it is resisted by shortsighted management. *One CFO once told me her organization didn't need succession planning because she wasn't going anywhere! She parted company with her organization shortly thereafter.* Succession planning isn't complicated but it is as complex as the potential talents of your organization's employees. It requires management attention and thought to be done successfully. *The organization's return on investment for taking the time and energy to focus on succession planning is immense.*

Succession planning requires an organization to

- *Identify its key management positions.*
- *Have the incumbents in these positions analyze the pool of talent available within (and outside of) their areas of responsibility.*
- *Identify potential candidates for promotion to these key positions.*
- *Detail how these potential candidates need to enhance their skills to be ready to be promoted to or assume the key positions.*
- *Have senior management review and approve the proposed succession and development plans, in partnership with human resources professionals who maintain and monitor the plans.*

Succession planning is performed annually; after the first cycle, the following annual plans are based on the database of talents already identified, with new hires and promotions included. To make this planning work, organizations must use the analysis gathered to ensure identified talents are developed appropriately, retained and promoted accordingly. Human resources has responsibility for managing and implementing succession planning. Human resources must be engaged in the ongoing dialogue in this process with all levels of management, exchanging and verifying information about the status, needs and progress of identified talents. The identified talents must be kept aware of their status for potential promotion and given active roles in their development.

Succession planning is a definite and clear statement of a work culture that practices what it preaches about valuing colleagues, committing to growth from within and respecting the contributions, potentials and ideas of the workforce.

This demonstrated commitment enhances the loyalty and morale of your colleagues and the organization's overall level of employee satisfaction. Such a commitment is a solid foundation for motivating employees' productivity in a mutually respectful work environment.

Managers foster the success of succession planning by

- *Being aware of the strengths and needs of teammates by practicing emphatic listening, being leaders and maintaining authenticity in the workplace.*
- *Understanding that leaders of successful teams hire, motivate and develop strong, talented teammates.*
- *Promoting and practicing the philosophy that teammates each bring unique strengths that may be in areas in which the leader is not as talented.*
- *Being motivated to work with talented dynamic colleagues and basing hiring and promotion decisions on that motivation.*
- *Seeing success at work as a team achievement, only possible if the team is talented and flexible enough to support each member and the joint effort simultaneously.*

In my senior year of high school, I was given advice that has been proven true every day of my work life. Robert Silverman, the vice chair of the social studies department at Samuel J. Tilden High School in Flatbush, Brooklyn advised me

"Always work with people smarter than you are. Find bosses who know more than you do and learn from them. When you're a boss, gather around you people who are intelligent and have commonsense, and who know more than you do. Let that be your reputation as a manager. Manage talent and your career will manage itself."

Recognition

Recognizing the efforts, achievements and successes of colleagues, teammates and teams is the single most cost-effective way to positively influence your workplace and build a culture for success. It starts with making recognition a part of your everyday duties. The many forms recognition can take in the workplace enable you to demonstrate your understanding and appreciation of the jobs being done with ease and flexibility. You can show recognition by stopping by your colleague's work area for a talk and saying how and what you recognize for praise; sending an e-mail or a voice-mail, especially effective at the beginning or end of the workday; taking colleagues to lunch or ordering lunch in for the team; sending a letter of appreciation to a colleague's manager for inclusion in the personnel file; writing a note that is delivered to a colleague's desk; recommending a colleague's efforts to a senior manager for a formal letter of appreciation from the organization; giving a teammate a special assignment; having a monthly employee recognition program; etc.

No matter which technique you use, recognition only works if it is sincere, specific, aimed in the correct direction and sufficient. One of the freight companies for whom I worked had an elaborate recognition program for its sales force, involving a "President's Club," financial rewards and an end of year dinner party. The sales force was well taken care of in the recognition department; however, what was being recognized was top line revenue, sales booked, not how profitable those sales became (or didn't become). This encouraged some salespeople to sell just about anything to anyone – services the company couldn't deliver at the price agreed on, contracts with new customers with shaky financials, incentives paid for business on which the company never collected payment.

The rest of the company knew this and the negative instances overshadowed the work of the sales folks that was profitable. Rather than a recognition program, most of the rest of the company viewed this as a misplaced effort that ignored the company's dire reality because no one else was recognized unless their work resulted in profitable business. The criteria for recognition, like the elements of the organization's compensation policy must be clear, sensible and understood. *Let the recognition fit the effort and accomplishment.*

Keep in mind a sliding scale of recognition techniques that cover small, medium and large achievements appropriately. A typed signed letter of thanks from the organization's president is higher up the scale than a handwritten note from you, although there are circumstances in which both are fitting recognition. There is one recognition rule overall - **"Discipline in private; praise in public."** This rule has been attributed to a number of people; however, I've heard it repeated many times long before any one attribution is dated. It's a truism that is always worth remembering. No one deserves to be reprimanded (or fired) in front of his or her peers and everyone appreciates appropriate public praise.

Discipline

You and I know fellow managers who dread having to discipline colleagues. Leaders and cultures are judged by how, why and when they discipline their teammates. Keep the elements of leadership in mind when faced with this task. Fair discipline, delivered respectfully and evenly is crucial to maintaining your team's morale and efficiency. If you can use discipline to motivate improved performance, you can achieve success.

The following list describes the key best practices to ensure your organization's disciplinary process is both effective and can withstand challenges from disciplined employees (and ex-employees) and from outside agencies (state unemployment division, human rights offices, etc.).

Like previously cited best practices lists, all of the elements must be in place and managed properly to ensure overall effectiveness. This usually requires management to review these practices regularly and modify how some elements may be being implemented, to account for cultural and organizational differences in workplaces.

Nine Elements of a Best Practice Disciplinary Process

1. *Establish the rules and make them clear. Don't expect your colleagues (or you) to know what is and isn't allowed in the workplace unless those rules have been thought out and documented.*

2. *Communicate the rules and train your team on them. Make awareness of the rules a component of the work culture. Distribute the policy handbook, get a signed receipt, post the key rules in the workplace, maintain a reference copy of the handbook at the ready, discuss the rules and have periodic refresher discussions with your team.*

3. *Be aware of the work environment and your team. You can be proactive only if you are attentive and involved in your team's daily activities.*

4. *Act in a timely manner whenever you become aware of a problem or potential problem. Hesitation in enforcing the rules = permission to break the rules.*

5. *Investigate all instances fully, with the assistance of other managers, supervisors and human resources professionals if necessary, and document your findings. Adhere to contract provisions in union settings.*

6. *Keep an open mind. Don't pre-judge. Recognize and filter personal feelings.*

7. *Provide due process. Let all sides have the fair opportunity to speak, with you listening. Ensure you and the colleague understand the problem.*

8. *Decide based on the factual evidence, not rumors and hearsay. If you cannot substantiate either side in a problem situation, instruct both sides that you will be monitoring as they go about their jobs in compliance with the rules.*

9. *Discipline fairly, ensuring the discipline fits the violation. Don't measure with a ruler and cut with an axe! Like situations require like disciplines. Minor offenses require suitable responses. Don't try to make an example of a teammate by disciplining him or her severely for an offense for which others have gotten off lightly. Have another manager or a supervisor with you to witness the disciplinary meeting. If a union member is involved, follow the Weingarten Rule and have a union representative accompany the employee.*

I've worked with a small handful of colleagues who were adept at pushing their managers' buttons. Because they could count on their managers' over-reacting to any situation, the button pushing worked and they were seldom disciplined appropriately. Managers who leap into disciplinary situations do themselves, their colleagues and their organizations no justice. Incendiary responses do not resolve problems. Take the time to consider and pursue the elements listed above and your response will be properly measured and effective. Indeed, in those situations in which a severe discipline is called for, your measured response will hold up under scrutiny and challenge.

I once experienced having to re-hire an employee terminated because she used the company's telephone system to place harassing calls to her supervisor 27 times in one day! The reason she had to be re-hired was an arbitrator's ruling that the manager who terminated her hadn't asked for her side of the story before firing her. He had made up his mind before she was summoned to his office. Now, his mind may not have been changed by whatever she claimed was her side of the story, but because he hadn't given her the opportunity to say her piece, the company got stuck with her again.

Some disciplinary situations may call for a cooling-off period before you decide and manage the appropriate response. You have the ability to say "You need to take a day (or the weekend) to consider what I've told you I've substantiated in this situation. When we get together again, I want you to tell me if you're ready to move forward from this and bring your performance back up to expectations." This is a viable technique to let the proposed discipline sink in and have real effect. Most union contracts allow management to suspend workers (send them home for the day) with pay, while managers investigate situations or work with shop stewards to craft the appropriate response.

How Do People Behave at Work?

I have observed four general types of workplace behavior: *Appropriate, Inappropriate, Violation of Policy and Illegal*. Each type of behavior has distinct characteristics and each type requires distinct responses and responsibilities for managers.

This line diagram, moving left to right, and the following notes illustrate regressive behaviors at work and managers' responsibilities in turn.

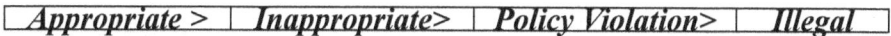

Appropriate >	*Inappropriate>*	*Policy Violation>*	*Illegal*

APPROPRIATE: Meets reasonable workplace behavior standards, follows Code of Conduct, in compliance with policy and law, is productive and contributes to group goals and organizational mission. *Examples* – punctual attendance, meets work deadlines, treats others respectfully.

Manager's Responses and Responsibilities – set standards; communicate applicable laws, policies, goals and mission; encourage, recognize and reward productive performance; provide feedback and support; evaluate timely; foster training and development opportunities; manage assignments and promotions.

INAPPROPRIATE: Does not meet reasonable workplace behavior standards but not in violation of policy or law, may be "one-off" behavior, neither severe nor pervasive, hinders productivity but doesn't have major negative effect on attaining goals or achieving mission. *Examples* – frequent lateness and missed deadlines, uncooperative attitude.

Manager's Responses and Responsibilities – Observe or learn about incident (do not rely on rumors, hearsay or second-hand reports); speak with parties involved; listen; assess characteristics of incident (previous occurrence/same parties?); address behavior; emphasize expected behavior; document incident (written notation for manager's reference); counsel; monitor.

VIOLATION of POLICY: Does not meet reasonable workplace behavior standards and violates policy, may be severe or pervasive, may be based upon a person's or persons' protected class status, impedes productivity, potentially harms team cohesiveness and trust, may be individually harmful, disrespectful or demeaning to team member(s), detracts from achieving mission, harms organization's effectiveness and image. *Examples* – Using epithets about race, gender, age, etc.

Manager's Responses and Responsibilities – observe or learn about incident(s); consult Human Resources and any designated reporting entity; investigate incident(s) thoroughly in partnership with Human Resources; speak with complainant (object of behaviors), listen and take notes and reassure that person the organization takes this seriously, it will be investigated promptly, information gained is managed on a need to know basis, there can be no retaliation for making the complaint, and results will be reported at the conclusion; speak with all involved parties, listen and take notes; give target of the investigation (person complained about) opportunity to relate his/her side of the story; share all information with appropriate entities (Human Resources, other reporting entity) on a confidential on a need to know basis; assess and analyze all relevant information gathered; determine extent of incident(s)/behavior(s) and whether this is repeated or similar to past situations; determine appropriate response; communicate response to complainant and target in summarized writing; implement any necessary organizational change; hold refresher sessions for work teams on policies; monitor affected parties and remain aware for any retaliatory actions.

ILLEGAL: Does not meet reasonable workplace behavior standards and violates policy and law, is severe and pervasive, may be based upon a person's or persons' protected class status, impedes productivity, potential to harm team cohesiveness and trust is high, likely harmful, disrespectful or demeaning to team member(s), detracts from achieving mission, harms organization's effectiveness and image, increases organization's vulnerability to regulatory oversight, governmental administrative proceedings and adverse legal action. ***Examples*** – workplace theft and drug use.

Manager's Responses and Responsibilities – Same as ***Violation of Policy***.

The Proactive Approach at Work

More important than knowing the best practices for delivering discipline is knowing how to avoid situations that require disciplinary action. Many of the following proactive approaches to avoid disciplinary situations are re-statements of best practices and ideas we've discussed previously. Successful management builds upon itself like sturdy blocks in a foundation.

This list, just like its companion on Best Practice Disciplinary Elements, needs to be in place and functioning fully to ensure success. It will not foster and enforce successful change if it is only paid lip-service and not managed actively. These Proactive Approaches must be seen as a budget plan for an effectively controlled work environment: a set of dedicated resources to promote a productive workforce and address problems before they become time and energy consuming disasters.

Proactive Approaches to Avoiding Disciplinary Situations
1. *Have an Employee Assistance Program, publicize it and use it.*
2. *Give timely constructive criticism to teammates and accept it from others.*
3. *Conduct exit interviews and give separated employees the chance to speak their minds about*

your organization from a former insider's point of view.

4. *Give your teammates straightforward information about the organization, the work and their performance regularly.*

5. *Ensure there is a clear mutual understanding between you and your teammates on your expectations of performance and behavior. This understanding is reinforced by relevant job descriptions and periodic performance reviews: discipline for poor performance should never come as a surprise. Moreover, few circumstances are more embarrassing to an organization than attempting to discipline a teammate for poor performance when the teammate's prior performance evaluations were positive.*

6. *Conduct pre-employment background checks and drug screens.*

7. *Coach teammates on skills improvement and mentor colleagues to accept greater responsibilities and promotions.*

8. *Be authentic. Live your values in line with your organization's values.*

9. *Listen and respond accordingly.*

The disciplinary situation that surfaces most often is absenteeism. Employees who are absent frequently or absent in a pattern (every Friday, the days after holidays, an extra day at the end of a vacation) tax their team's productivity and take advantage of their co-workers. Frequent absenteeism signals a major problem within your team and it must be dealt with and stopped immediately. In organizations that are subject to Family and Medical Leave Act provisions, always offer FMLA coverage and encourage your colleagues to utilize this protection for legitimate situations. FMLA is not a cover for laziness, indolence or deceit. The best practice administration of FMLA in an organization requires staff, management and human resources to cooperate in documenting and monitoring the legally provided time away from work.

Chronic absenteeism by one colleague erodes the unity and credibility of the entire team effort. Everyone on the team must know the organization's absence policies. As the leader, you must enforce these policies in an even, fair and timely manner. You must monitor your teammates' adherence to these policies. I give the same message on attendance to every team with whom I work – we are adults and colleagues, therefore, I trust we can manage our time professionally and collegially; when you have needs due to exceptional circumstances, tell me and we can devise a plan to deal with these exceptions; if I have to monitor any one person's time then there is a bigger problem involved and we will resolve that problem swiftly.

Where a teammate is absent or late repeatedly without prior consultation and approval by you, that behavior must be dealt with firmly. Talk to that person immediately upon his or her return to work and have that conversation in private.

The elements are;

1. *Review the applicable policy and your knowledge of the situation. Check for any application of FMLA, disability coverage, uniform services or reserve duty, childcare issues, or organization policy for jury duty or court appearances.*
2. *Ask about and learn the person's reasons (and motivations) for the absence(s) or lateness(es). Is there another, underlying situation that must be resolved?*
3. *Discuss the person's current attendance situation and what that means in light of the applicable policy.*
4. *Establish an action plan – no more occurrences for the remainder of the year; a doctor's note for any subsequent occurrences; referral to FMLA or disability; a verbal warning; a written warning; suspension; termination; etc.*
5. *Ensure you are both aware of what is expected going forward, especially the potential disciplinary response and consequences.*
6. *Inform the person that you are documenting this meeting in writing and including it in the personnel file.*

You must then monitor the situation and follow through on what has been discussed. Be consistent in applying the attendance policy for your team. As with all policies, your successful management is dependent on fair and honest discipline, not the mistaken desire to "make an example." The only example that is successful is wise leadership. Be timely in addressing incidents and implementing your action plans. Understand that your silence or inaction in these instances undermines your leadership, weakens your team's spirit and productivity and encourages others to defy the rules. *On the other hand, fix an underlying problem and regain a loyal co-worker.*

The opposite of absenteeism is presenteeism, being at work when you shouldn't. It isn't heroic to come to work dripping flu germs and infect everyone around you. Teammates who are sick with contagious illnesses or who need to be away from work to recover sufficiently must be kept out of the workplace for reasonable amounts of time. This reasonable time is covered by sick leave, FMLA, disability, leaves of absence and other programs in the workplace. Your organization's sick leave policy should be flexible enough to reasonably cover limited absences for caring for dependents (in instances where the FMLA provisions do not apply). Provide the tools (laptops, telephone lines) and your support for occasional telecommuting (working from home via information networks), as required.

After a recent snowstorm, the federal Office of Personnel Management reported a 29% daily recovery of productive time during the storm due to telecommuting workers.

Separation

As we and our teammates live through work, there are times when we must part company. When better opportunities surface outside the organization, the parting is bittersweet. While you regret the organization couldn't hold a valued teammate, it is best that colleagues feel and know they can advance or change their careers with your blessings and support. You just don't know when a departing colleague will become a returning colleague with fond memories of how he or she was treated by the separating organization. *Best practice performance evaluation, employee development and discipline programs, along with a respectful workplace, minimize the losses of valued colleagues.*

Firing disruptive employees quickly does more to improve organizational culture than almost anything else management does.

Organizations generally request resigning employees to give reasonable notice before leaving. This is usually only a request, not an enforceable policy. The doctrine of at- will-employment works more effectively in the employee's favor in this situation than in the organization's in a termination. Employees working under an employment agreement may be required to give adequate notice, if that notice is reasonable in length and the agreement provides adequate consideration for such notice (a 90-day notice period, for example, during which the departing employee is paid salary.)

Your organization must have in place an exit strategy for all employees. This strategy addresses the separation basics of

- A checklist to ensure organizational property is accounted for and returned; passwords, keys and files are returned to management; physical and virtual accesses are turned off; and proper paperwork is filed.
- COBRA coverage is offered appropriately.
- An exit interview is conducted, an exit interview form is sent after separation, or an exit interview by telephone is arranged.

Conducting exit interviews is a best practice. The exit interview leaves the departing colleague with the understanding that his or her observations about the organization are important. It is a source of significant feedback about the organization, from persons willing to share their opinions and experience in a safe setting. This significant feedback is as important coming from separating staffers as it is from departing managers. The exit interview may uncover a previously hidden problem or a potential problem. An employee who felt intimidated or coerced by a manager during the employment tenure, will likely feel less constrained to voice these feelings after the separation. Any expression by the separating employee of discriminatory, unfair or illegal treatment during his or her tenure in the organization must be acted upon as quickly and surely as if that person was still an employee. The law and your policies still apply and your thorough investigation will be the basis for your defense if that separated employee decides to pursue legal action after leaving. The exit interview must be documented.

What questions do you want to ask in an exit interview? What first attracted you to join this organization? Did you receive fair opportunities for development and if not, please explain? How has your opinion of this organization as a workplace changed and if so, how and why? Were the organization's policies and work rules explained to you clearly and followed by management and if not, please give details? What factors influenced your decision to leave this organization? What attracts you to your new workplace? Would you consider working for our organization again and why? Would you recommend our organization to a friend as a place to work and why or why not?

I've had the experience of a separated colleague attempt to rescind a resignation. Always get resignations in writing. Never permit a separated employee to rescind a resignation. If you can't get the resignation in writing, meet with the person, discuss in detail why that person is resigning and then immediately document your conversation. This must be a consistent practice in the organization.

If you must terminate a colleague's employment, do it with respect. A termination must never come as a surprise. It must be the final action in a set plan that honestly establishes, communicates, monitors and evaluates that person's job performance and adherence to the organization's policies.

During the course of this plan, you keep your colleague fully informed of your expectations and the attendant consequences for both success and failure.

You document the steps and progress along the way. You meet with and discuss the progress on a regular and appropriate schedule. You listen to discern how he or she is progressing and if there are any underlying problems that are impeding success.

Your empathic listening is an important part of due process for that colleague. He or she must know the status of the plan, what is or isn't being done properly, and that you are paying attention. *Respect the fact that it is a rare occurrence when a teammate wants to fail – that person may not understand what is needed for success or may not have the skills to attain it, but almost always the desire to succeed is present.*

Your leadership abilities are necessary to support *and* constructively criticize that person to have the best opportunity to turn around a non-performing or under-performing situation.

This set plan should be embodied in a *Performance Improvement Plan (PIP)*. A *PIP* is a written document that is shared with the employee as the method by which he or she can improve performance. It is retained by you and the employee as an agreement, referred to through the schedule set for the plan, as a reference. It is written by you, with assistance from human resources and any supervisors involved in this employee's work. A *PIP* has *five* detailed sections:

1. *What I expect from your performance.* This is a list of specifics for all the duties, deadlines, behaviors and policy expectations. The reference documents for this section are the job description, performance evaluations, the policy handbook and any management notes in the personnel file.

2. *What I have observed and has been reported to me.* "On two occasions I have received complaints from customers about your service delivery and these complaints have been substantiated." "Your teammates report that you allow your phone to ring off the hook when you are at your desk." "You have been observed screaming at fellow employees on two occasions."

3. ***What you need to do to perform up to expectations.*** "Answer your phone after three rings consistently." "Adhere to all organizational policies when dealing with your colleagues, the public and customers." "Respond to customer requests within 24-hours of receiving them."

4. ***How I will be monitoring and managing your improvement.*** Detail any training or coaching to be delivered. Set a schedule for how long the *PIP* will be in effect and when you will be meeting with that person to discuss progress. A *PIP* should contain a reasonable time frame, appropriate to the improvements sought, generally two weeks time to 30- , 60- , or 90- days. You must meet with the employee on a regular schedule of at least once a week, often more like twice a week.

5. ***What will happen if the improvement does not occur in the specified timeframe.*** Usually, this means termination. Extend a *PIP* in the rarest of circumstances when substantial but not total improvement has been achieved and then only for an extra week or so. This is not a permanent process.

The object of the **PIP** is to salvage the teammate, not to provide the groundwork for termination. (It costs *75%* of a non-manager's salary to replace an employee and *150%* of the salary to replace a manager. It pays to take every step to keep a teammate.) When improvement does not occur, a **PIP** does build the termination groundwork. At that point, the termination is a conclusion, not a surprise.

Termination of Employment

When termination is called for, it is your leadership responsibility to conduct the separation meeting with the employee. This must be done in the privacy of an office or a conference room. Always have a fellow manager, supervisor or a member of human resources accompany you and act as witness. In union settings, have a union representative accompany the separating employee and you must ensure you have followed all contractually required steps. If you have reason to be believe the separating employee may become violent, alert your organization's security function and consider having someone from security either present in the room or standing by in physical proximity.

I once conducted a separation meeting with a colleague (not from my team) who was known to boast about his "biker" image. His manager was located in Europe so I was asked to accompany the manager and actually conduct the meeting (because of my knowledge of U. S. employment practices and policies). I asked a senior security manager to sit in on the meeting – he was as tough professionally as the separating employee was known to be intimidating. When we sat down, the separating employee stated he had no idea why his employment was going to be terminated. He had been given numerous documented warnings and a PIP, none of which he followed. He remarked, "I'm a Marine." In a quiet but firm voice, the security professional told him, "I'm a Marine too and you're well aware of why we're here today." The separating employee was quiet for the rest of the meeting and left work without incident.

Separating employees may express disbelief during the meeting. In a simple, straightforward way remind them of what led up to the separation and what has been documented. Tell them that at this point, a separation is what is best both for them and the organization. Detail any severance and final pay due; in some states final pay must be given to the separating employee immediately, so it's best to do it during the meeting as a positive element. Allow the employee to talk and vent, so long as it is done peacefully but do not give in to requests to reconsider the separation. The decision has been made after much consideration and opportunity for improvement. Point the person to the future. Allow the employee to remain in the room or go to another area for privacy at the end of the meeting. Have someone from human resources or an outside counseling firm available for the employee to go to next to talk about subsequent steps (including COBRA coverage, unemployment insurance, EAP assistance, etc.). If this is part of an overall reduction in force, have a counseling firm's representative on hand in another room to talk to the separating employee.

Give the separating employee time to pack his or her personal effects or to make an appointment to do so. Look the person in the eye, shake his or her hand, give a wish for success apart from the organization and inform the person that an exit interview will be conducted.

When the meeting is concluded, check your list to ensure all of the organization's steps have been followed. Alert your computer and security folks to end access permission. ***Ensure you and your colleagues refrain from any negative comments about a separated employee.*** Denigrating a former colleague is disrespectful, damaging to the work environment ("If they talk that way about what's his name, I wonder what they say behind my back?"), and potentially legally actionable.

In certain situations, during mass layoffs or when separating a longtime employee or senior manager, you and human resources should consider a mutual separation agreement that provides severance pay in return for a waiver of claims against the organization. Remember that filing claims of discrimination and giving evidence to the EEOC cannot be waived because the government's right to combat alleged discrimination is greater than the employer's right to do away with potential problems.

A mutual separation agreement, especially with employees over the age of 40, must contain explicit timeframes for the employee to review the terms, consult with counsel and revoke the agreement. This type of agreement must be drafted by the employer's legal counsel and administered by human resources. In these situations, the cost of an agreement can easily be justified as much less than the cost of fighting a contested separation.

For both managers and staff who are separated, management should weigh the costs of contracting for transition counseling (to assist separated employees with confronting their situations, dealing with their families and friends, and re-entering the job market) against the benefits of helping former colleagues, showing a commitment to practicing the organization's values even in tough times, and improving the organization's reputation in negative circumstances. The separated employee, no matter how failed his or her performance, is still a fellow human being and a former colleague. *The honesty, fairness and respect you demonstrate in these situations must be no less than what you do everyday to lead by example and live your values.*

Managing Yourself

For all the care managers must exercise with their teams at work, managers must care for themselves as well. Start, of course, by having faith and respecting who and what you are: your life, skills, and your place in your profession are gifts. You owe yourself the dignity of appreciating who you are in the workplace and the insight to enhance your ability to lead your team by managing your own life properly.

Best Practices –

- o *Having a healthy sense of humor.* Sincere laughter can ease a heavy load of responsibilities. Laughing is a proven and delightful method of releasing stress-reducing, healing forces inside of you. We are given the ability to laugh at birth, long before we can fully understand irony and pathos. Our sense of humor used judiciously can defuse a tense situation, disarm potentially angry colleagues and assist us in breaking through others' defensive barriers. When we laugh sincerely at our own foibles and quirks, use a smile to invite discussion, and humorously admit to our own mistakes in front of others, we can weather just about any storm with our sanity intact. It is easier to laugh than to cry, to smile than to frown. The work world is serious; it mustn't be grim. Our colleagues appreciate us more when we can stand as equals and share the appropriate honest humor of a situation.

- o *Keeping everything in context.* Managers who scream and otherwise act-out in the workplace, have an unhealthy sense of themselves. Their life is out of balance. Their faith is absent. Personal authenticity requires us to have a viewpoint about ourselves that is consistent with and

177

in proportion to the reality of the workplace and our colleagues' valid points of view. So the first knowledge is to appreciate and understand that our duty is to respect our creation. Managing our teams honestly, respectfully and authentically follow from that.

o ***Relying on family and friends to keep the parameters of our life real and sound.*** These are the people who connect us to this earth. A healthy self needs a healthy foundation – in the workplace and the home. Whenever I feel pressed down by the weight of my work, I take a long look at the photographs of my children and nieces and nephews, the people to whom this book is dedicated. Each of their faces is full of wonder and promise. My friend Rosemarie reminds me that our children are loaned to us from Heaven. One day we will leave this earth and, we pray, our children will live on to carry our faith into the future. I have gained sound insight from my parenting experience, watching my children and listening to what they have to say. I am blessed with friends of quality; confidants whose loyalty and generosity of spirit make me become a better person. Managers must be grounded by relationships with people like these in order to work with and lead others successfully.

o ***Understanding there is no difference between "life" and "work."*** Ensure your life outside of the workplace is full of pursuits that help you grow – exercise, reading, hobbies, keeping a diary or journal, social and cultural events, and quiet times. All work is only half living. We've heard it said that someone's mind is only on work: it's just the opposite because that person is only using part of his or her mind. Work occupies one part of our intellectual and emotional capacity. We are capable of and ready for much more and that much more will enhance our capacity for work. We need to use that capacity or risk losing it. I carry with me a leather-bound diary for making notes about topics of interest as I come across them. The act of keeping these journals has sharpened my attention to my work and improved my ability to listen properly to my thoughts. I try to take a 20 to 30 minute walk at lunchtime every day – the stress relief of physical exercise is proven and it is long lasting. Managers require regular, reliable stress relief mechanisms that are built into their workday, to maintain their focus. The only folks without any stress are the ones who are in the next life now. For the rest of us, stress is a given – it is our responsibility to manage it as a blessing, not a curse.

o *Taking responsibility for our life and how we live it.* It's up to us: who we are every hour of every day is our responsibility. One of my colleagues, Soledad called me and discussed the different styles that managers we've known have displayed in the workplace. Soledad remarked that the characteristic she appreciated most in a particular manager was his liveliness. She elaborated, "The glow in his eyes as he spoke told me he wasn't **just** a professional. This was a special person, alive, awake, aware, engaged, focused, interested, intelligent, ready to listen, eager to assist. That is what I appreciated." This manager understood that he was responsible for himself and how he interacted with others. He wasn't going to sleepwalk through life. That understanding began with his taking care of his own life.

To be mentally healthy, we must
- ✓ Listen more than we speak
- ✓ Read regularly on a wide range of subjects and viewpoints
- ✓ Be thoughtful and interested about the world
- ✓ Articulate our thoughts civilly, in writing and the spoken word
- ✓ Remain curious, enthusiastic and thankful about life
- ✓ Learn something new about ourselves and others, with each new experience.

To be physically healthy, we must

   ✓ Be physically active and exercise on a regular and consistent basis (use the stairs instead of escalators and elevators; park in the spot farthest from the entrance; walk, hike, jog, run, swim, work-out, play competitive sports, etc.)

   ✓ Practice moderation through sensible eating and balanced living – do nothing to excess; relax, but don't be lazy; eat but don't overdo; compete but don't obsess

   ✓ Make our own health one of the priorities in our life, consistent with our faith and values, with appropriate attention (doctors' visits, healing time, prayer, etc.)

   ✓ Take the lessons gained through keeping our life in context and apply them to leaving workplace issues at work and home life issues at home; give ourselves appropriate time for rest, reflection and prayer.

Nobody's Fault: Your Responsibility

The easy route on the wrong path in our journey blames everyone else for our own problems. We earn an inadequate salary not because we haven't developed our skills or we don't control our spending, but because someone else in our organization earns more than we do. We're not promoted because someone else is prejudiced against us, even though the person promoted has worked diligently for the opportunity. Our life is unfulfilled and unhappy because someone else is making it that way. We can't do our jobs successfully because someone other than ourselves won't let us. These attitudes lead to failure quickly. *Life is not ours to be miserable spectators.*

When we make mistakes in or outside of work, we are responsible for acknowledging them, accepting the proper consequences, resolving the issues and learning from our errors. We ask to be forgiven for our trespasses, as we must be ready, willing and able to forgive those who trespass against us. *The bottomline is, living successfully requires our faith, self-determination, conscious action and responsibility for how our life is lived.*

In this regard, there is one term I have not employed: self-esteem. There is nothing intrinsically wrong with this term. The original connotation of "self-esteem" that I remember from my upbringing denoted self-satisfaction, authentic self-appreciation, self-criticism and humble pride. The current usage I find is characterized by false pride, absence of self-criticism, antagonism for others' criticism, a smug self-deception that our own happiness is paramount to living our life authentically, and a pointless self-centerness. The terms we need to describe how we regard ourselves are respect and self-respect. They are mutually requisite. ***Honest self-satisfaction is a result of our governing our own life through our faith and values.*** Self-esteem is not a license for us to believe and act as if misguided self-satisfaction is either the only object of life or life's primary aim.

Lesson:

"If you don't understand that you work for your mislabeled 'subordinates,' then you know nothing of leadership. You know only tyranny." Dee Hock, founder of Visa

Chapter Eleven

The Last Word

Believe.

At every single point in my life, and there have been many, when I have been in doubt about my future, anxious about my present, approaching personal crisis, deep in self inflicted confusion, and unsure about why I needed to move in a certain direction, I have been shown concretely the path of belief. I can say this without hesitation or fear of contradiction – *Believe.*

If I summarized this book in one phrase, that phrase would be

Believe in yourself, in the dignity and worth of others, and in a Creator much greater than you who gives life, compassion, a conscience, dignity, strength, resiliency and values in this world.

With this belief you can move mountains. Without it, you will be lost – living your life, maybe even materially prosperous, but lost nonetheless – empty and unfulfilled. It took a near fatal car accident in which my life could have ended in the merest fraction of a second but was saved, to make me understand that I live in a world of purpose. In that world I am on my own journey to fulfill my purpose for being alive.

Faith, belief, prayer, respect and compassion are among the mightiest tools you possess.

No one and no thing, not an organization, a bully, a mob, an army or a government can take away those tools. I said at the beginning of this book that I have faith in you and that you already have the tools you need to be a better, more successful person and manager. Everything we have discussed in this book should lead you back to that affirmative conclusion.

Fear and failure are passing. Faith, belief and success are enduring.

Believe all things are possible because they are – all of human history proves that. Printing ideas on paper, traveling around the globe, broadcasting messages instantaneously, harnessing electrical and nuclear power, seeing a thought become an action and changing the world – *all things are possible.*

He and our faith in Him are life's truest constants.

The work world continues to change. Where once our parents and their parents and the generations before them trusted the organization or company to drive their careers, now we must drive our own careers. We have the choice of where we will work, for whom, and how our work will effect our own life, our family's life and the lives of our colleagues. There is no separation between our life at work and the person we are before and after work. We must now be entrepreneurs of our own careers.

We are the instruments of change. Whether we accomplish change and are successful in a small group or a great mass, it is up to us. **There is a Jewish saying that advises us to pray as if everything is up to God and act as if everything depends on us**. Both courses of action require courage, faith and persistence.

You will encounter resistance to your persistence. The opponents of belief aren't skeptics; skepticism requires room for belief. Healthy doubt is valuable for strengthening belief and keeping it honest. The enemy of belief is cynicism.

> **"The cynic puts all human actions into two classes – openly bad and secretly bad."**

Cynicism ridicules belief; its purpose is to destroy the ability to believe. Cynicism kills trust. Put cynicism out of your life. Ban it from the workplace.

Earn your colleagues' trust by believing in them and they will believe in you. Baffle the forces of resistance by showing them respect and believing that you are capable of working with them successfully – by example you will win over some of them and outwit the rest! The person convinced against his or her will is of the same opinion still, so don't attempt to sway others with your words primarily – keep your thoughts simple, honest and direct – but show others how you square off against adversity by being your authentic self. **"Well done is better than well said"** advised Ben Franklin. Your demonstrated self-respect will garner the respect of others, including many who don't agree with you on a host of issues. The seducer uses sugar coated bullets to try to succeed. *It is the depth of faith, logical compassion and intelligence in your actions that will succeed.*

Stay guided by your faith. Occasionally, you will stumble. We all do. By faith you will not stumble headlong: pick yourself up and move that rock on which you tripped.

> *Successful management* "without failure is like religion without sin: It doesn't work." Paraphrasing Professor Allan Meltzer of Carnegie-Mellon University

Lethargy, insincerity, deceit and the differences between what is right and what is wrong may get in your way. *Moral choices are not relative decisions.* Right and wrong are not relative terms – recognizing the difference can be starkly simple or vigorously complex but faith will lead you to the path of success. Trust in the power of your simple determination to overcome obstacles. The Greek mathematician Archimedes stated that **"with a place to stand"** he could move the Earth. *Faith is that place to stand. Faith is the best practice.*

You will not be alone in exercising your beliefs. Your faith unlocks your inborn ability to do what is right and be successful. As I meet new people, each new relationship reveals the reservoir of belief that nourishes them. That reservoir is huge.

Almost every day now I meet people, some for just fleeting moments, and know instantly that they are Believers. Recently I was at a highway rest stop and lingered to look at sunglasses. After 15 seconds of conversation with the salesman I said "You're Born Again, right?" He was and he wondered how I knew so quickly! On a dinner cruise recently, I spontaneously volunteered to take a photo of the two couples seated near my table. Standing with the two husbands from that group later on the ship's deck, it took all of one minute for me to ask "Are you Born Again?" Of course they were, having just returned from a mission trip to their native countries! On a phone call with a potential consultant for one of my clients, approximately three minutes into the call the consultant confirmed my observation that he too was Born Again. It is as if it is His plan to always bring Believers seemingly casually into my life, just to keep teaching me a lesson.

In the largest study ever conducted on unconventional medical approaches, the U.S. government found that 43% of adults use prayer as an alternative medical therapy. **Upwards of 92% of all Americans are Believers.** You will find people of faith all around you, if you stand ready to respect and work with them. *If you feed your faith with belief, your doubts will starve.*

You are blessed. Blessings happen every day. We need only to be ready and able to see, appreciate and use the blessings in our lives. I look at my children, family, friends, the opportunities I've had and continue to have, my modest talents and skills, the great colleagues I've had the chance to get to know, the lessons I've learned, and I see how blessed I am.

My friend Laura observes wisely that she knows people in her life who are very blessed with health, material comforts and loved ones, but these people are the most miserable because they lack the light to see their own blessings. *Look around you. The blessings are everywhere you are.*

Where does non-belief lead, where does one give thanks for a day lived fully, a child's birth, the glorious mystery of the infinite universe, the gracious assistance of a colleague? You don't need the experience of a near-fatal car crash to remind you that life is a present that is given for a purpose. *Live life with a grateful heart and you will see and appreciate your blessings every day.*

> "Lord thou hast given so much to me;
> Give one thing more – a grateful heart."
> George Herbert

As you and I now part, I wish you the success you work for and deserve. I hope I have helped you – maybe one story I've told or one point I've illustrated has been relevant to your experience and will stay with you. I am now at the point in my life where the most rewarding parts of living are watching my children grow, loving those around me and helping my colleagues find the greatness, goodness and success that they possess. If I've assisted you in your journey, I've succeeded. Now that I have passed on to you the thoughts and ideas in which I believe, share your life with your colleagues. When your days darken, as they will from time to time, use that source inside of you to guide yourself and those with you. *And give thanks.*

Managers have a special duty at work. *To be responsible for leading colleagues to success is an honorable mission and a rewarding job.* I've heard it said that what modern organizations don't do well is to train managers in how to manage people, to listen and understand their co-workers. *I believe that's true but I also believe managers who look within themselves with prayer and a sense of conscience will find those skills and much more.*

Our Creator's great gift of life includes providing us with everything we need to live to the fullest, if only we will seek Him, believe and follow.

You will know that you are on the right path on your journey when

- ✓ *Your colleagues seek you out for advice and genuinely appreciate when you listen.*
- ✓ *You feel a sense of pride and purpose when you think about your work, outside of the workplace.*

- ✓ *You see colleagues who have worked with you, excel and move forward in your organization because you encouraged and mentored them.*
- ✓ *Others tell you that you've made a difference in their lives.*
- ✓ *One of your most noteworthy personal traits is your strength of character.*
- ✓ *You face each challenge with a strong and positive faith.*
- ✓ *The clarity of your decisions is a hallmark of your leadership.*
- ✓ *You give thanks each and every day for the blessings of your life.*

In the end, each life has meaning and purpose – we must uphold the value of each life and our own life as precious.

I believe in you.

Lesson:

"I know that in my heart that man is good, that what is right will always eventually triumph and there is purpose and worth to each and every life." Ronald W. Reagan

APPENDIX

Employment Law Overview

Federal Laws

- The Civil Rights Act of 1964 is discussed in the chapter.
- The Fair Labor Standards Act (**FLSA**) was enacted in the 1930s. It has been amended numerous times since then. One of its most important purposes is to define which workers are classified as "exempt" and not eligible to be paid overtime for hours worked over 8 per day or 40 per week (states use one of these two methods for calculating overtime) and which are "non-exempt" and eligible for paid overtime. Generally, managers, qualified professionals (doctors, lawyers, certified accountants, etc.), and workers who use "independent judgment" to perform most of their duties are classified as "exempt" and not eligible for paid overtime. "Non-exempt" workers must be paid at the overtime rate (usually 1.5 times the regular salary rate) for any overtime worked. They cannot be given "compensatory time" (extra paid time-off) for overtime worked. You need to know how your team members are classified; if the classification has been reviewed recently; that you have pre-approved all overtime to be worked and the specific work to be done on overtime; and that the approved overtime worked is recorded in the payroll system and paid on time. If you attempt to use side arrangements to give "non-exempt" team members time-off in lieu of overtime pay or you try to accumulate and bank their overtime pay as a lump sum paid out in a delayed manner, you will be breaking the law. The consequences of doing this are severe. You really

don't want the force of the government swarming over your payroll records, do you? Additionally, there should be a poster describing the prevailing minimum wage in or near your workplace.

- Equal Employment Opportunity (**EEO**) is the term for a set of laws that prohibit employers from hiring or making any employment decisions (raises, promotions, terminations, transfers, consideration for assignments, evaluations) based on protected class characteristics. There are three basic types of EEO discrimination. **Disparate treatment** involves intentionally treating workers in different protected class groups differently (deliberately hiring only white males as managers, for example). Sexual harassment can, and often does take the form of disparate treatment. **Adverse Impact** involves employment practices that have a negative impact on a protected class group, either intentionally or unintentionally (searching for qualified job candidates without recruiting in areas or through sources that reach out to protected class jobseekers, as an example). **Past effects** involve employers continuing employment policies and practices that perpetuate past discrimination. For example, a long established minimum height requirement for a particular job (this has been cited most notably in instances of firefighter positions) is not intentionally discriminatory but it may unfairly limit female jobseekers.

- The Americans with Disabilities Act (**ADA**) prohibits employers from making employment decisions based upon a person's or persons' qualified disability, as defined by law. Both alcoholism and substance abuse, if established by treatment and known by the employer, can qualify as disabilities covered by ADA. This is the primary reason that managing an employee suspected of substance abuse must be done carefully, working with a human resources professional. The ADA mandates that employers notified that an employee has a qualified disability (usually by a medical practioner's written statement) must make "reasonable accommodations" for that employee to obtain treatment and continue employment. Judging what "reasonable accommodations" are can be difficult. The construction of a ramp to allow employees in wheelchairs to have access to a building is a reasonable accommodation. Allowing an employee being treated for a qualified disability to have a flexible schedule, that doesn't otherwise seriously affect the business, to receive treatments is reasonable. Creating a desk job in a warehouse, in which no desk jobs existed previously, to accommodate an employee who can no longer perform the duties of a warehouse worker, is not a reasonable accommodation. Similarly, you cannot ask a job applicant if he or she has a disability but you can ask,"Is there anything that would prevent you from performing the entire range of duties required in this position?" The ADA requires case-by-case management, with human resources, of each relevant situation. The Rehabilitation Act of 1973 basically extends the ADA to federal agencies and contractors.

- The Family and Medical Leave Act (**FMLA**) has been adapted and modified by many states. Its basic requirement is that certain employers (based on employee population) must provide specific amounts of unpaid leave to certain employees (based on length of employment) for the following events – the serious medical condition of a child, spouse, person under guardianship or parent; the employee's own serious medical condition; or the birth or adoption of a child. During this unpaid leave, the employee must be continued on medical benefits (with the employee continuing to pay appropriately if required) and given back his or her job or a similar job upon return. FMLA is a difficult and complex law to manage. States have varying modifications of the amount of leave that is granted. There are often conflicts with overlapping disability coverage. Employers may elect to require employees on FMLA to use up all of their paid leave (vacation, personal days and sick time) as part of the leave granted. Employees are responsible for proper notice of FMLA requests and employers are responsible for making employees aware of FMLA's availability. Employers may challenge an employee's claim of a qualified serious medical condition.

- Even some state government administrators of FMLA (labor departments) aren't sure what is and isn't a qualified serious medical condition. A common cold, for example, by itself isn't a serious condition but a common cold that triggers an asthmatic attack is one. Managing FMLA always requires a human resources professional's assistance.

- The Occupational Safety and Health Act (**OSHA**) mandates standards and requirements for workplace safety and conditions. It is too voluminous and complex to summarize here adequately. Yet its provisions touch almost every workplace. OSHA deals with hazardous materials, warehouse structures, ventilation and other safety and health situations. It has recently been applied to workplace violence situations concerning the employer's obligation to provide a safe place of employment and to do what is reasonable to protect employees' lives, safety and health. Make sure your organization, usually through its human resources function, enforces and monitors OSHA compliance. There should be an OSHA poster displayed in or near your workplace.

- The Age Discrimination in Employment Act (**ADEA**) prohibits discriminatory employment practices based upon a person's age, with the designated starting level as 40 years of age. The Older Workers' Benefit Protection Act (**OWBPA**) amends ADEA to protect employees age 40 and above from discrimination in employee benefits plans and severance agreements.

- The Pregnancy Discrimination Act (**PDA**) applies to private employers with 15 or more employees, and prohibits discrimination against pregnant women. Among other provisions, it mandates that a woman may not be denied employment solely because she is pregnant; a pregnant woman on leave due to her pregnancy has the same return to job rights as her co-workers on disability or sick leave; and a pregnant woman able to perform her job may not be required to take a leave of absence. An employer may not discipline, demote or fire a pregnant employee simply because of her pregnancy.

- The Immigration Reform and Control Act of 1986 among other things requires employers to obtain **I-9 Forms** and valid proof from employees to ensure they are legally able to work in the U.S.

- The Health Insurance Portability and Accountability Act of 1996 (**HIPAA**) prohibits discriminatory employment practices based upon an employee's or employee dependent's existing medical condition. The element of this law that will likely effect you the most as a manager is the requirement for organizations to ensure health related information (doctor's notes, insurance claims, etc.) is kept confidential – this usually means purging employee records of these documents. There are significant penalties attached to breaching this confidentiality. It is best to refer any questions about an employee's health to the human resources function. HIPAA requires the organization to have a health information privacy policy, a procedure for complaints, and a description of how the organization protects employee privacy when using and disclosing health information.

- The Comprehensive Omnibus Budget Reconciliation Act (**COBRA**) mandates that terminated employees must be provided the opportunity to continue their health insurance coverage for a specific time after leaving the job. These COBRA benefits are usually administered by a vendor through your human resources function. Former employees have to pay a market rate insurance premium to the insurance carrier, if they choose to continue their coverage.

- The Employee Retirement Income Security Act (**ERISA**) establishes and enforces standards for employee benefits programs, such as mandating employees receive summary plan descriptions (SPD) that detail what the benefits plan provides and how it operates.

- The Uniform Services Employment and Re-employment Rights Act (**USERRA**) prohibits discrimination in employment against members of the armed services, including the National Guard.

- The Equal Pay Act requires that men and women in the workplace receive equal pay for jobs that have **equal skills** and **equal responsibilities**. Be aware that jobs with the same titles do not necessarily trigger Equal Pay Act protection. The two-part test of skills and responsibilities is necessary to make that determination.

- We've discussed the Fair Credit Reporting Act (**FCRA**) previously. The Fair and Accurate Credit Transactions Act (**FACT**) amends FCRA concerning investigations of employees performed by third-parties (vendors, law firms). FACT eliminates the requirements to notify employees of these investigations, seek their consent, and disclose the resulting investigative reports. Investigations covered by FACT are for suspected misconduct related to employment or for compliance with laws, organizational policies or self-regulatory rules.

Creditworthiness investigations are not covered by FACT. FACT protects employees' privacy rights by mandating that third-party investigation findings may be disclosed to the employer, a government agency, a self-regulatory authority, or as required by law, only. Employees involved in such investigations may be given a general summary of the findings.

Common Law

- The doctrine of **employment-at-will** is a common law concept that in certain circumstances, absent an employment contract or agreement, allows employers to terminate a worker's employment at any time (so long as there are no discriminatory reasons or causes) and allows employees to end their employment, at any time. Enforcing employment-at-will, as you might imagine, can be a complex and potentially danger-laden legal situation. Numerous federal statutes limit employment-at-will, including the Bankruptcy Code, the Railroad Safety Act and the Clean Air Act. Always obtain human resources and legal assistance if you are looking at the application of this doctrine.

- The doctrine of **constructive discharge** is a potential cause of civil action for an employee who has resigned due to the employer's deliberate intolerable conduct that any reasonable person could not endure at work.

- Three of the doctrines of negligence that apply to managers are **negligent hiring, negligent retention,** and **negligent supervision**. These doctrines have evolved in our common law over time and are used in legal actions to characterize mismanagement that results in some harm. Negligent hiring refers to employers who knew or reasonably should have known about an employee's unfitness for the workplace before that employee was hired (hiring a convicted thief in a job that requires trustworthiness, who then steals from other employees). Negligent retention may be used if an employer becomes aware an employee should not be retained but does nothing about it (continuing to employ someone who commits a violent act in the workplace). Negligent supervision refers to management's failure to more closely monitor an employee's actions (having evidence that a particular employee may be responsible for attacks on other employees but not monitoring that employee's actions in the workplace).

ENDNOTES

Henry Ward Beecher quoted in "The Secrets of Life Power" by Barry B. Gallagher, 2008, Nightengale Press, pg. 57

Andrew Imparato quoted at Slate.com Dec. 12, 2004

Prologue

George Harrison quoted at Prabhupada News, Oct. 8, 2009
"On a wire and a prayer," Dan Dakin, June 15, 2012, Niagara Falls Review online
"Faith at Work," Russell Shorto, Oct. 31, 2004, New York Times Magazine, pg. 42
"Faith at work poses challenges," Anne Thompson, March 23, 2005, MSNBC.com
Laura Nash, Harvard Divinity School, quoted in "Religion in the Workplace: The growing presence of spirituality in Corporate America," Michelle Conlin, Nov. 1, 1999, Business Week online
George Harrison quoted at Interview Henley-On-Thames, Oxfordshire, 1982

The First Word

Mercedes Ellington quoted in "Public Lives: Musical Royalty Gazes Back to Beginnings," Chris Hedges, June 3, 2004, New York Times, pg. B4
"Miracle Rabbi," Neil Graves, March 22, 2004, New York Post, pg. 23
"Tale of Courage," Leonard Greene, April 20, 2004, New York Post, pg. 29
"Science or Miracle?; Holiday Season Survey Reveals Physicians' Views of Faith, Prayer and Miracles," Dec. 20, 2004, Businesswire.com
"Religion in the Workplace: The growing presence of spirituality in

Corporate America," Michelle Conlin, Nov. 1, 1999, Business Week online
"Alicia's Message," Anne Ryder, Dec. 2010, Messenger of St. Anthony, pg. 30

"What I'm saying is . . . "

"Fleeting Beauty," Ben Stein, Feb. 2011, American Spectator, pg. 64
"Soul Training," Alexandra Gill, Dec. 12, 2003, The Globe and Mail, pg. C1

You are the Leader

Alasdair Philip, Nov. 21, 2003
"The Civil War," Geoffrey C. Ward, Ric Burns and Ken Burns, 1990, Random House, New York, NY, pg. 271
"Thought for Today," May 25, 2006, Today in history: May 25, MSNBC. com
Terry Ebert, Feb. 20, 2011
"Risky Business: James Bagian – NASA astronaut turned patient safety expert – on Being Wrong," Kathryn Schulz, June 28, 2010, Slate.com
Dr. Samuel Johnson quoted in Boswell's "The Life of Samuel Johnson, LL.D.," 1791
"Rational Mysticism for a Young Movement," Max Borders, Dec. 20, 2012, The Freeman online
"Sexual Harassment," Michael Barrier, Dec. 1998, Nation's Business, pg. 3 (Burlington Industries, Inc. v. Ellerth, U.S. Supreme Court, No. 97-569, 1998; Faragher v. City of Boca Raton, U.S. Supreme Court, No. 97-282, 1998)
Clara Knopfler quoted at Congregation Sons of Israel presentation, April 2004
"Level 5 Leadership," Jim Collins, Jan. 2001, Harvard Business Review, pg. 87
thinkexist.com, attributed to President Harry Truman and Ralph Waldo Emerson

Authenticity

"Hamlet," Wm. Shakespeare, Act I, scene 3, lines 78-82
"Consultant's Corner," Joe Tomaselli, Spring 2004, Ayers Report, pg. 7
"The Power of Resilience: Achieving Balance, Confidence, and Personal Strength in Your Life," Drs. Robert B. Brooks and Sam Goldstein, 2004, Contemporary Books, Chicago, IL
"Secrets of the Happy Life," John Langone, June 22, 2004, New York Times, pg. F7
Hubblesite, "Team Hubble: Servicing Missions"
"History Lesson," Angus Wilkie, June 2012, Architectural Digest, pg. 91
"Laurance Rockefeller Memorial Tribute," MSKCC Center News, Jan. 2005, pg. 13
"Hamlet," Wm. Shakespeare, Act III, scene 4, lines 206 and 207
"Poor Richard's Almanack (1733-1758)," Benjamin Franklin, U.S. State Department website
"Sophie Scholl – The Final Days" (2005), directed by Marc Rothemund, written by Fred Breinersdorfer
Alasdair Philip, Nov. 22, 2003
"Not So Undercover Boss," Lois Weiss, Oct. 20, 2010, New York Post, pg. 39

Listening

"Sister Carrie," Theodore Dreiser, 1900, Random House, New York, NY, Chapter 1 online
"The Reflective Practitioner, How Professionals Think In Action," Donald Schon, 1983, Basic Books, New York, NY
first-thoughts.org, Jan. 5, 2013, relating President Nixon anecdote
"The Psychopathology of Everyday Life," Dr. Sigmund Freud (Translated by A. A. Brill), 1901, T Fisher Unwin Limited, Bouverie House Fleet Street
"Leaders Ponder Role of Religion in Conflicts," Mary Fowles, Dec. 14, 2003, The Gazette Montreal, pg. IN3
"12 Angry Men (1957)," directed by Sidney Lumet, written by Reginald Rose

thinkexist.com, Einstein quote

"Catholic Update Guide to Vocations," Mary Carol Kendzia series editor, June 2012, Franciscan Media, Cincinnati, OH

"The New Man," Thomas Merton, 1961, Farrar, Straus & Giroux, New York, NY, pp. 151-152

"Reliance on Technology is Changing Human Society," Gabriel Kates-Shaw, ACT-SO essay 2012

Respect

"Fear in the Workplace: The Bullying Boss," Dr. Calvin Morrill, June 22, 2004, New York Times, pg. F1

Lee v. Curt Manufacturing Inc., No. 03-C-523-C, W. D. Wisconsin 2004

"At U.N., a Missourian Who Wears Faith Boldly," Warren Hoge, July 1, 2004, New York Times, pg. A13

"Story Time," Alfredo Molina, June 2004, InStore Magazine, pg. 100

Ed Feulner, Hillsdale College commencement address 2004, quoted by Michele Malkin, May 4, 2005, Jewish World Review online

Out in the Open

"Regulating off-duty conduct: How far can you go?," Nov. 2004, The HR Specialist, pg. 1

"Lessons From the Master," Coeli Carr, March 21, 2004, New York Post, pg. 32

"Think your co-workers are on drugs? They are!," Paul Tharp, July 23, 2004, New York Post, pg. 37

"Alcohol kills more than AIDS, TB or violence," Stephanie Nebehay, Feb. 11, 2011, MSNBC.com

O'Connor v. Ortega, U.S. Supreme Court, 480 U.S. 709 (1987)

NLRB Memorandums OM 11-74 (Aug. 18, 2011), OM 12-31 (Jan. 24, 2012), and OM 12-59 (May 30, 2012), Office of the General Counsel

"The Minister's Black Veil," Nathaniel Hawthorne, 1836, University of Virginia Library, Electronic Text Center

The Law

Meritor Savings Bank, FSB v. Vinson, U. S. Supreme Court, 477 U.S. 57, 1986

Oncale v. Sundowner Offshore Services, U.S. Supreme Court, 523 U.S. 75 (1998)

"Alleged Discrimination Costs $12.1 Million," HR Reporter, March 1999, pp. 1 and 8

Kenney v. Wal-Mart Stores, 100 S.W. 3d 809, 817 (MO 2003)

"Black Police Officer Sues Over Noose," May 9, 2000, APBnews.com

Frederickson v. Olston Health Services, Inc., May 1, 2001, HighBeam Research.com

"Documentation: Making sure it can't be used against you," Jan. 10, 2003, What's Working in Human Resources, pg. 1

Andrew Carnegie quoted at WorldofInspiration.com

Warren Buffet quoted at "Trust Is a Must," Chris Sandlund, Oct. 1, 2002, Entrepreneur.com

Andrew Carnegie quoted in What's Working in Human Resources, Jan. 10, 2003, pg. 8

Dennis Harvey v. Maytag Corp., U.S. Court of Appeals, 7th Circuit, No. 03-3409, July 23, 2004

EEOC v. Sundance Rehabilitation Corporation, No. 1:01 CV 1867, N.D. Ohio 2004

Nestler v. Chartwell Dining Services, No. 02-CV-1115, N.D. NY, 2004

IBM Corp. (June 15, 2004) NLRB

Mathias v. Phillips Chevrolet, Inc., 269 F. 3rd 771, 2001 U.S. App. Lexis 21879 (7th Cir. No. 00-1892, Oct. 15, 2001)

U.S. Department of Labor, Bureau of Labor Statistics, Census of Fatal Occupational Injuries

U.S. National Institute for Occupational Safety and Health

The Survey of Workplace Violence Prevention, Bureau of Labor Statistics, Oct. 2006

"Workplace Violence: First Line of Defense Facilitator's Guide," 1994, Coastal Human Resources, Virginia Beach, VA, pg. 35

U.S. EEOC Change Statistics, FY 1997 Through FY 2012

Hillig v. Rumsfeld 2004 U.S. App. Lexis 18260 No. 02-1102 (10th Cir. Aug. 27, 2004)

The Center for Values Based Leadership, Sacred Heart University, Fairfield, CT

The Value of Values

"The Ordeal of Change," Eric Hoffer, 1976, Buccaneer Books, Inc., Cutchogue, NY, pg. 3
"Groundwork of the Metaphysics of Morals," Immanuel Kant, 1785
"Gallup's Discoveries About Great Managers and Great Workplaces," Marcus Buckingham and Curt Coffman, March 15 – 22, 1999, TheWorkplaceColumn.com
"Perk Up," Samuel Greengard, Jan./Feb. 2004, Arrive, quoting Laura Sejen of Watson Wyatt, pg. 10
"Corporate Culture," HR Reporter, March 1999, quoting Henry Brull, pp. 1 and 6
"Risky Business" ibid
"Devil's Radio," George Harrison 1987

Work, Life Best Practices

"Saint of the Day, June 6th," June 6, 2012, Franciscan Media online
El v. SEPTA, 479 F.3d 232 (3rd Cir. 2007)
Wilson v. B/E Aerospace Inc., No. 03-14909, 11th Cir., 2004
"10 questions to avoid in job interviews," June 2004, You & The Law, pg. 7
"Telework cuts federal government's losses during D.C. area snowstorms," Joe Davidson, March 25, 2010, The Washington Post online
"The high cost of turnover," Employee Recruitment & Retention, 2004, pg. 9
"Exercise may make you a better worker," Jacqueline Stenson, June 14, 2005, MSNBC.com
"Subordinates," Employee Recruitment & Retention, 2004, pg. 9, quoting Dee Hock

The Last Word

"Lectures to Young Men: On Various Important Subjects," Henry Ward Beecher, Lecture IV, (1860)

"Poor Richard's Almanack (1733 – 1758)," ibid

Book Review "Why Capitalism," Bruce Yandle, Jan./Feb. 2013, The Freeman, quoting Allan Meltzer, pg. 35

thinkexist.com, Archimedes quote

"More Than One-Third of U.S. Adults Use Complementary Medicine, According to New Government Survey," National Institutes of Health NCCAM Press Release, May 27, 2004

"More Than 9 in 10 Americans Continue to Believe in God," Frank Newport, June 3, 2011, Gallup.com

Laura Longmire, Dec. 7, 2004

George Herbert quoted at Goodreads.com

"First a Private Farewell, Then a Public Outpouring," Charlie LeDuff and John M. Broder, June 8, 2004, New York Times, pg. A23 (Inscribed on the western side of President Reagan's crypt)

ABOUT THE AUTHOR

Anthony E. Shaw is a seasoned professional of over 35 years in senior management and human resources leadership positions. He has worked in almost every business sector; Government, Private and Public Companies, Not-for-Profits, and Entrepreneurships, including starting and managing his own consulting business, Anthony E. Shaw Consultants, Inc.

He delivers leadership development courses to hundreds of potential organizational leaders and conducts training for hundreds more on workplace law, HIPAA and customer service in healthcare, the workplace diversity of 7.1 billion people, listening to manage, human resources for doctors in practice, managers' best practices, and other topics.

Along the way, he founded the first internal control unit in the New York City Department of Investigation; worked with the FBI and other law enforcement agencies to unravel the Parking Violations Bureau scandal; served as the first Deputy Mayor of African-American heritage in Yonkers, NY; guest lectured at Berkeley College, NY; presented at the Institute of International Bankers; and assisted a wide variety of clients in resolving employee complaints and proactively addressing problem areas in organizations large and small.

His roster of clients includes:

- The Institute for Family Health
- Apple Direct Mail Services
- Abbey National Treasury Services plc U.S. Branch
- The Birch Wathen Lenox School
- The Brooklyn Music School.

He has served on the boards of:

- The Green Chimneys School, Brewster, NY
- STRIVE of Fairfield County, CT
- The Ethical Community Charter School, Brooklyn, NY.

He is a member of the Society for Human Resource Management, the Foundation for Economic Education, the Eagle Forum, and the Federalist Society, and a graduate of Bernard M. Baruch College of the City University of New York, magna cum laude. He is the recipient of the 1994 YWCA African-American Heritage First Award.

He is married to Bonnie Kuang and they have an energetic toddler, Ethan Anthony Reagan. Anthony's daughter, Emma Rose Pernell Kates-Shaw attends Swarthmore College and his older son, Gabriel Victor Carleton Kates-Shaw attends Ossining High School and Lagond Music School.

Anthony and Bonnie live in Scarsdale, NY, where they give thanks every day for their blessings.

ACKNOWLEDGEMENTS

There are simply too many people who have blessed me with their wisdom and guidance over the last four decades for me to be able to acknowledge and thank each one by name.

My mother Edna Lorraine Pernell Shaw and my stepfather Carleton Shaw set my path with love, understanding, humility, intelligence and gratefulness to God. Along with my brothers, LeRoy, Carlton, Jr. and John, they prepared me to face the world with a prayer of thankfulness always in my heart.

Fred and Paula Kleinfeld have kept me as close as one of their own children for nearly 30 years; guiding, counseling, sometimes admonishing, but always with parental love and to them I am grateful.

My wife Bonnie and my three wonderful children, Emma, Gabriel and Ethan, hold me steady in awareness of God's great Love, in the face of the headwinds of a less than prayerful world. To them, my eternal love and thanks.

I've worked with real professionals every step of my journey. To all those I worked for and with in Dun & Bradstreet, the General Services Administration, the New York City Department of Investigation, the Office of the Mayor of the City of Yonkers, Danzas/AEI, Abbey National Bank, the Institute for Family Health, and Apple Direct Mail Services, I say thank you. Many of you are cited in this book. Special thanks to my friend and client Jeffrey Meyer, whose constant encouragement, more than any other single person except my wife, made this book possible.

I am especially thankful for having served in the administrations of two very wise, honest and decent mayors, the late Edward I. Koch of New York and the Hon. Terrence M. Zaleski of Yonkers. You are both shining examples of the best of public service and you taught me more by your examples than I could ever learn from a graduate course of study.

With only one extraordinary exception, the managers for whom I've worked have been honest, caring, mentoring leaders. I am most grateful for the opportunities to have worked for Hans Toggweiler and Robert Ferrari, gracious gentlemen who demonstrated their commitment to my profession and lived their values.

I thank Kristen Tetrault, Dr. Terry Ebert and Cherie Roberts for their critical review of the manuscript and their astute comments. Keith Pearson and Ryan Ratliff of Aventine Press patiently led me through the publishing process and contributed their creative expertise – thank you.

I have been fortunate to work with some of the finest business consultants in the work world today – my thanks to all my colleagues at the Ayers Group, Frenkel Benefits, Gateway International Group, Associated Benefit Consultants, and Benchmark. My special thanks to Dr. David Burnham of the Burnham Rosen Group for his sage counsel.

My thanks to the hundreds of participants I've trained and helped develop based on the principles and lessons contained in this book. You taught me far more than I did you.

Most importantly, I am ever grateful that my Redeemer Liveth!

www.ingramcontent.com/pod-product-compliance
Lightning Source LLC
LaVergne TN
LVHW011225080426
835509LV00005B/326